JEWISH NEW YORK

To those who came,
and in memory of those they left behind.

JEWISH NEW YORK

Notable Neighborhoods and Memorable Moments

BY IRA WOLFMAN

PHOTO RESEARCH BY RONDA SMALL

UNIVERSE

Half title page: Kids posing on Ludlow Street on a quiet day during the waning years of the Lower East Side as a Jewish residential area, 1934.

Title page: Young women drawing at the Educational Alliance Art School. c. 1920s.

First published in the United States of America in 2003 by

UNIVERSE PUBLISHING
A Division of Rizzoli International Publications, Inc.
300 Park Avenue South
New York, NY 10010
www.rizzoliusa.com

Copyright © 2003 Ira Wolfman

2003 2004 2005 2006 2007/
10 9 8 7 6 5 4 3 2 1
Printed in the United States of America
ISBN: 0-7893-0643-3
Library of Congress Catalog Control Number: 2003104742

Editors: Ellen Cohen and Elizabeth Ferber
Designed by Paul Kepple @ Headcase Design
www.headcasedesign.com

ACKNOWLEDGMENTS

Ira Wolfman and Ronda Small wish to thank the following institutions and professionals who so generously shared their time, advice, and materials with us: Photographers Richard Berenholtz, Leni Sonnenfeld, and Harvey Wang. Archivists, curators, executive directors, and private collectors Robin Bernstein and Ilene Morales at the Educational Alliance; Elizabeth Block; Muriel Borin and Martin J. Frankel; Marlene Brill; Gertrude Felberbaum; Joan Gordon at US/Israel Women to Women; Leo Greenbaum and Erica Kaplan at YIVO; Norman Goldberg at Yeshiva University; Shelley Helfand at the American Jewish Joint Distribution Committee; Marybeth Kavanagh and Julie Viggiano at the New-York Historical Society; Madelyn Kent at Old York Library; Alvin and Barbara Mass; Bonni-Dara Michaels at the Yeshiva University Museum; Joshua Eli Plaut of the Center for Jewish History; Sarina Roffe at the Jewish National Fund; Peter Schweitzer and his remarkable collection of Judaica; Steven W. Siegel at the 92nd Street Y; Lyn Slome, Sarah Davis, and Susan Woodland at the American Jewish Historical Society; Rickie Weiner at the Jewish Theological Seminary; Marlene and Bud Wertheim; and Steven Wheeler at the New York Stock Exchange. And a very special thanks to Barbara Cohen and Judith Stonehill, sine qua non. . . .

CONTENTS

Ellis Island, New York.

(Above) Ellis Island in the early 1900s. The Hebrew Immigrant Aid Society (HIAS) helped the new Jewish arrivals.

The Jews of New York City today make up the largest, richest, most creative Jewish community in the world. Yet little more than a hundred years ago, most of them were desperately poor, living in teeming immigrant neighborhoods. How these Jews—through struggle, education, and determination—transformed themselves and their city is a great American success story. Jewish New Yorkers powered major city businesses such as the garment and media industries, reinvented the Broadway theater, and helped invent the modern labor movement. They also won Nobel Prizes and introduced the United States to such delights as pastrami, egg creams, and an inimitable form of Jewish comedy.

But this community saga did not begin in the twentieth century. The first Jews arrived in New York City in 1654, when it was a tiny outpost called New Amsterdam, ruled by a peg-legged tyrant named Peter Stuyvesant. He did not want to let the first Jewish immigrants stay, and only relented after being ordered to do so by his superiors in Holland.

Over the next 350 years, Jewish New Yorkers helped finance the construction of Trinity Church, fought in the Revolutionary war, sold $200 million in bonds to help the Union pay for the Civil War, and underwrote much of the building of the American railroad industry. And four New York Jew-

שפּײַז װעט געװינען די קריעג!
אידער קומט אהער צו געפינען פרײהײט,
יעצט מוז אידר העלפען זיא צו בעשיצען
מיר מוזען די עלליעס פערזאָרגען מיט װײץ.
לאָמען קײן זאַך ניט גײן צו אין גוזוען.

יעניטעד סטײטס פוּד פֿערװאַלטונג.

(Above) "Food Will Win the War!" proclaims this 1918 Yiddish-language poster.

ish boys even grew up to be world-champion boxers! *Jewish New York* offers a brief portrait of this resilient community of Jews— where they settled, how they earned a living, what they ate and drank, how they supported the less fortunate, where and how they prayed—and highlights the places of interest in Jewish history of the past and present. The book also explores the surprising diversity of the Jews who populated this world-from the original Sephardim, to the influential German-origin "Our Crowd" Jews, to the Ladino-speaking Jews from Turkey and Greece who shared the Lower East Side with the hundreds of thousands of Yiddish-speaking Jews from Eastern Europe.

For nearly 350 years, New York City has been home to this uniquely American Jewish community, and this uniquely Jewish American community. Here, in celebration, is a piece of their story.

(Above) Lifting her lamp beside the golden door: the Statue of Liberty greeted over two million Jewish immigrants from 1883 to 1924. Photograph by Richard Berenholtz.

Birds Eye View of New York City.

(Above) Crowded by so many imposing buildings today, lower Manhattan and its adjoining harbor had a more inviting air during the early part of the twentieth century.

JEWISH LANDMARKS

✦ and ✦

NEIGHBORHOODS

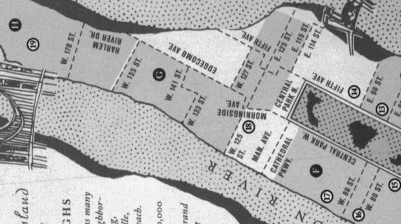

Manhattan Island

OTHER BOROUGHS

BROOKLYN: *Home to as many as a million Jews. Key neighborhoods include Williamsburg, East New York/Brownsville, Flatbush, and Brighton Beach.*

BRONX: *As many as 400,000 Jews have lived here, in communities such as the Grand Concourse, South and East Bronx, and Riverdale.*

QUEENS: *Middle-class Jewish enclaves such as Forest Hills and Kew Gardens have now seen an influx of Jews from former Soviet nations.*

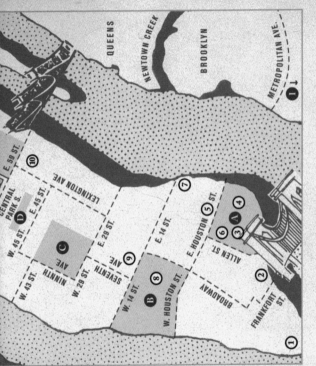

LANDMARKS:

1. *Museum of Jewish Heritage*
2. *Shearith Israel Cemetery*
3. *Eldridge Street Synagogue*
4. *Educational Alliance*
5. *Katz's Deli*
6. *Kossar's Bialy Bakery*
7. *Second Avenue Deli*
8. *Hebrew Union College*
9. *Center for Jewish History*
10. *Central Synagogue*
11. *Park East Synagogue*
12. *Temple Emanu–El*
13. *Jewish Museum*
14. *Mount Sinai Hospital*
15. *Shearith Israel Synagogue*
16. *Zabar's*
17. *B'nai Jeshurun Synagogue*
18. *Jewish Theological Seminary*
19. *Yeshiva University*

NEIGHBORHOODS:

A. *Lower East Side*
B. *Greenwich Village*
C. *Garment Center*
D. *Diamond District*
E. *Upper East Side and Yorkville*
F. *Upper West Side*
G. *Jewish Harlem*
H. *Washington Heights*
I. *Williamsburg*

REV GERSHOM MENDES
SEIXAS
1746 ~ 1816
ERECTED BY THE MANHATTAN CHAPTER

Chapter One
THE PEOPLE OF JEWISH NEW YORK

"There are many Jews settled in New York. . . . They have a synagogue and houses . . . they enjoy all the privileges common to the other inhabitants of this town."

—PETER KALM, A SWEDISH VISITOR, 1748

"There are German Jews, Spanish and Portuguese Jews, Jews from Holland, Galicia, Hungary, Rumania, and the Ukraine. . . . There are multi-millionaire Jews of Riverside Drive, the poor Jews of Harlem, the Bronx and Brooklyn."

—PAUL MORAND, C. 1930

Who are the Jewish New Yorkers? There are no simple answers to the questions of when Jews came here, where they came from, or what position in society they hold, economically and socially. Currently, one million Jews live in New York City; in the 1950s, the community reached two million. Those numbers make New York the largest Jewish urban community in history. But Jewish New York is not only enormous, it is also enormously complex. The substantial size of New York's Jewish society is personally significant to every Jewish person who lives in the city. The presence of so many Jewish people allows the populace to live free from the self-consciousness that often inhibits Jews in other cities.

Jews came here from many countries and brought with them diverse customs and traditions. Since the 1830s, diversity has always characterized New York Jewry. Except for two experimental periods, no organization has had jurisdiction over all of New York's Jews. The freedom that comes with that lack of centralization—to be the kind of Jew you wish to be, in concert with others who feel the same way—helped create the community's vitality and its magnetic pull on the rest of the Jewish world.

(Opposite) Jewish D.A.R. members, 1932. The Phillips and Nathan families gather in Congregation Shearith Israel's 1680s cemetery, in lower Manhattan, around the tombstone of Shearith's first Reverend, Gershom Mendes Seixas.

The great majority of New York's Jewish population is descended from the "World of Our Fathers" Eastern European immigrants. They flooded the Lower East Side and have subsequently enriched the city and country with their drive, humor, and creativity. This group forms the heart of the Jewish community in New York City. But these immigrants came to a city that already had known Jews for hundreds of years. Jews arrived in New York in historical waves, each group paving the way for the next. The Jewish value of "responsibility for one another" played an important role in helping newcomers to succeed. New York City's multicultural population—in which no one ethnic or national group dominates—also has been vital in creating a hospitable environment for Jewish life to flourish.

"Something about New York . . . has given rise to a pluralism within Jewish life that never before existed," Rabbi Arthur Hertzberg once noted. "A certain spirit of American live-and-let live. . . pragmatism . . . has made it possible for all kinds of Jews to live together not only in one city but in one community."

IN THE BEGINNING

The first group of Jews arrived at the tip of Manhattan in 1654 from South America. They were Sephardim, descendants of the hundreds of thousands who had been expelled from Spain and Portugal during the Inquisition, starting in 1492. Some left Spain for Turkey and the eastern Mediterranean. But the twenty-three who arrived in New Amsterdam were from families that had eventually settled in Holland after the expulsion. These Spanish and Portuguese Jews prospered under the relatively tolerant Dutch and, in the early 1600s, hundreds of them went to Dutch colonies on the northeast coast of South America, including the settlement of Recife, Brazil.

(Above) Grace Mears Levy, c. 1728. Second wife of Moses Levy, a prominent merchant and leader of New York's 75-family Jewish community in the early 1700s. Portrait attributed to Gerardus Duyckinck.

In early 1654, a colonial war between the Portuguese and Dutch ended in latter's defeat. Dutch settlers had to leave for other Dutch colonies or Holland. The ship carrying four Jewish men, two women, and seventeen children, however, was waylaid and eventually ended up in New Amsterdam. Exhausted and with little money for the continuing journey, the Jews asked to stay. Director-general Peter Stuyvesant was not agreeable. He wrote to the Dutch West Indies Company in Holland, requesting that "the deceitful race . . . be not allowed to further infect and trouble this new colony."

However, there were Jewish directors on the West Indies Company board and they interceded, noting Jewish loyalty and service to Holland. In 1655, this reply from the Company was sent to Stuyvesant: "We would have liked to . . . fulfill your wishes . . . that these new territories should no more be infected by the Jewish nation." But, they continued, that would not be fair to the Jews who had supported Dutch colonization. As a result, "These people may travel and trade to and in New Netherland and live and remain there, provided the poor among them shall not become a burden to the company . . . but be supported by their own nation."

The twenty-three became the founders of Shearith Israel, the still-extant, oldest Jewish congregation in North America (its grand synagogue is now on Central Park West in Manhattan). Stuyvesant did not allow Jews to pray publicly, but did grant them permission to buy land for a cemetery. The second Shearith Israel cemetery, with tombstones dating to 1683, can still be visited today on Chatham Square in Chinatown.

By 1664, the English had taken over New Amsterdam and renamed it New York. Jews were given more freedom, and in 1730, Shearith Israel built its first synagogue building on Mill Street (south of today's Wall Street). During the next 100 years,

(Above) Major Mordecai Myers, c. 1813. A longtime member of Shearith Israel, New York City's first Jewish congregation, Myers fought in the War of 1812 and studied military tactics under one of Napoleon's officers. Portrait by John Wesley Jarvis.

Jewish immigration was minimal with some Sephardim arriving from England and Holland. Others, the Ashkenazim (Germanic) journeyed from the German lands, Poland, and Russia.

FROM POOR GERMANS TO "OUR CROWD"

Larger numbers of German-speaking Jews arrived beginning in the 1820s through the 1850s, leaving Germany predominantly because of harsh anti-Jewish laws. But these Jews still felt a deep connection to German culture, and happily settled in a lower Manhattan neighborhood filled with non-Jewish Germans and known as "Kleindeutschland" (Little Germany). Years later, after those residents had moved uptown, part of this neighborhood would gain a new name: The Lower East Side.

Many German-Jewish immigrants were poor and found work as peddlers. But over a twenty- to forty-year period, a good number became wealthy. Calling themselves "Our Crowd," they became the city's assimilated German-Jewish aristocracy. Men such as Felix Warburg, Joseph and Jesse Seligman, the Bloomingdale Brothers, Isidore and Nathan Straus, and Jacob Schiff now owned banking houses and department stores. Others were successful clothing manufacturers. They looked, dressed, and felt American; even their synagogues had become more American and less European.

A FLOOD FROM EASTERN EUROPE

In 1881, revolutionaries assassinated Russia's Czar Alexander II, thrusting Russian society into chaos. Pogroms (anti-Jewish violence) broke out across the Russian Empire, and many thousands of Jews were killed. Subsequently, a flood of Jewish individuals and families fled Russia, Poland, Lithuania, Austria, Hungary, and Romania, and came to New York.

Following in the steps of earlier Jews, they settled on the Lower East Side. But these poor Eastern European Jews did not

(Above) Famed financier Felix M. Warburg led Kuhn, Loeb and Co. to become one of the world's great investment banks.

look, dress, or sound like Americans. Instead of German, they spoke the Eastern European Jewish dialect, Yiddish, and most followed old-world religious customs. Some came with a passion for socialist politics, others developed it later on.

New Yorkers of other ethnic backgrounds found these newly arrived Jews exotic and unnerving. Their foreign behavior was nothing like the culture of the assimilated, more established "Uptown" German Jews. These Jews, who believed that Christian New York had generally accepted them, now felt their hard-won status shaken. Not insignificantly, anti-Semitic incidents did increase during this period in New York City and around the United States.

Thankfully, leaders arose in the German Jewish community who stressed their responsibility to their coreligionists. These uptown "Hebrews" spent much time, money, and effort building institutions to uplift—and Americanize—their downtown cousins. The aid was generous, but often perceived by "downtown" Jews as arrogant and condescending. Misunderstandings affected both groups and many hurt feelings took decades to heal.

(Above) *In the Steerage*, George Luks, 1900. From 1881 to 1924, millions of "Russian"—more accurately, Eastern European—Jews endured trips in the depths of steamships from Bremen and Hamburg.

SELIGMAN, JOSEPH (b. *Baiersdorf, Bavaria, 1819;* d. *New Orleans, La., 1880),* financier, civic lead... man. Brother of Jesse Seligman; father of Isaac N. S... Emigrating to America, 1857, he served... some time as secretary to Asa Packer. He foun... clothing firm with his brothers including Jesse, which was transformed early in 1862 into the... ing house of J. & W. Seligman & Co. Strong s... ers of the Union, the Seligmans promoted lar... of U.S. bonds in Frankfurt at a time whe...

almost impossible to sell the national sec... England or France. During the presidenc... Grant, Joseph Seligman was one of his c... financial advisers, and throughout the 187... figured prominently in the conversion an... of the obligations of the United States. J... man was also active in New York City... and was a member of the Committee of S... ousted the Tweed Ring.

JOSEPH SELIGMAN
1817-1880
FINANCIER

Gussford
288 Fifth Ave., N.Y.

...G ROOM, HARMONIE CLUB, 10 EAST 60TH ST., NEW YORK.

(Above left) Joseph Seligman was a founding member of New York's German-Jewish "Our Crowd" aristocracy. He began as a peddler in 1837. By 1860, he was head of an international investment banking firm. (Above right) Dining room of the elegant Harmonie Club, founded by wealthy German Jews in Jew York in 1852.

McKim, Mead & White, Architects.   Wurts Bros. Photo.

ARCF&o 15, 1906

(Right) Levantine Jews on Delancey Street. The Abraham family of Salonika, Greece,
came to the Lower East Side in the early part of the twentieth century.

TURKS AND OTHER LEVANTINES

In the early 1900s, a much smaller group of poor Jewish immigrants also arrived on the Lower East Side—from Turkey, Greece, the Balkans, and Syria. Many of them spoke Ladino, a Jewish dialect of medieval Spanish that they had brought with them from Inquisition Spain to their homes in the eastern Mediterranean. For 400 years, these Jewish communities lived in relative isolation in the towns and cities of the Ottoman Empire such as Salonika, Greece, and Smyrna (now Izmir), Turkey.

Between 1900 and 1925, upheaval swept the area as Greeks and Turks fought wars, the Turkish army began seeking Jewish draftees, and the Ottoman Empire disintegrated. About 40,000 Sephardim left for America, most settling in New York and living on the East Side. They had difficulty connecting with Yiddish-speaking Jews, who found it hard to believe the new immigrants were Jewish. The Ladino-speaking Jews also had turbulent relations with their Uptown cousins—the Sephardim of Shearith Israel, at least some of whose roots went back to the

same Spanish and Portuguese heritage. The mostly affluent and assimilated Sephardim were wary of their impoverished Levantine counterparts. As with the Yiddish and German Jews, the more affluent offered help to the less fortunate, but resentment and misunderstandings often accompanied that aid.

REFUGEES AND ESCAPEES

The overwhelming flood of arrivals stopped in 1925, when restrictive new immigration laws took effect. However, Hitler's Nazism trapped millions of Jews in Europe, leading the United States Jewish community to begin relief and rescue efforts. They managed to transport only a small number people—perhaps 100,000 German Jewish refugees—here from 1936 to 1943. After the disaster, American Jews managed to bring another small number of concentration camp survivors—again, about 100,000—to the United States.

Today, nearly eighty years since the end of the greatest migration of Jews to New York, the city still welcomes Jewish immigrants from all over the world. And although many Jewish New Yorkers have moved to the suburbs or other parts of the United States over the past thirty years, many others have arrived.

A new wave of Eastern Europeans Jews began revitalizing many New York City neighborhoods during the 1980s, with approximately 200,000 Jews from the former Soviet Union settling here over the last twenty years. The immigrants included Jews from Uzbekistan and Tadjikstan, Russia, Belarus, and Ukraine. Several decades after World War II and the establishment of the Jewish State of Israel, a significant number of Jews from Israel also began settling in the New York City area. Today New York's Jewish community—this great Jewish melting pot—shows no signs of losing either its variety or its vitality.

(Left) "Young Russian Jewess, Ellis Island," photograph by Lewis Hine. By 1905—the date of this photo—New York had become the city with the largest Jewish population in the world.

Chapter Two
JEWISH GEOGRAPHY:
East Side, West Side, and Lower East Side

New York City has had many colorful and memorable Jewish neighborhoods: Harlem, Yorkville, Williamsburg, East New York–Brownsville, the East Bronx, the Grand Concourse, Washington Heights, and the Upper West Side. However, the most recognizable district and the one central to any story of Jewish life in New York is the legendary Lower East Side.

The name alone evokes a visceral world of sights, sounds, and smells: hundreds of thousands

of determined, hard-working Jews squeezed into dark, decrepit tenement buildings; streets of impossible density punctuated by pushcarts and swarms of people; overburdened mothers and fathers

painstakingly constructing, piece by piece, their children's, and grandchildren's, American dream.

The Lower East Side stretched from the East River to Houston Street, from Pitt Street to the Bowery. Key thoroughfares such as Orchard, Hester, Delancey, Rivington, and Grand were outdoor stages for the ongoing drama of the immigrant experience. By the early 1900s, the neighborhood's boundaries extended along Second Avenue, which became "The Yiddish Rialto," filled with theaters and shops.

In the Jewish geography of the East Side, immigrants from particular countries tended to settle around specific streets. Jews from

(Above) Shoppers examine 25-cent bargains in front of an Orchard Street storefront proclaiming "Kosher Tsiken Market" in Yiddish. Photograph by Andreas Feininger, 1940.
(Opposite) Hester Street was "the pushcart center of the East Side," wrote novelist Anzia Yezierska. "The air reeked with the smell of fish and overripe fruit."

Austrian Galicia ("Galitzianers") congregated between Houston and Broome on Pitt, Attorney and Willet streets. Romanians lived on the most congested streets: Chrystie, Forsyth, Eldridge, and Allen, south of Houston. Hungarians settled above Houston and east of Avenue B. The rest of the East Side was filled with Russian, Ukranian, and Polish Jews.

Rutgers Square (later renamed Straus Square after philanthropist Nathan Straus) was a neighborhood gathering place, filled regularly with protestors, labor rallies, and election-night gatherings. Directly on the square was the nine-story home of one of the community's great institutions—the *Forverts* newspaper, the *Jewish Daily Forward.*

On the corner of Essex and East Broadway was the famous Garden Cafeteria, where kibitzers and critics, writers and artists met, argued, debated . . . and drank tea. At the square's east end loomed the great red-brick Educational Alliance, a cultural outreach institution founded by German Jews in 1893 for their East-

ern European brethren. And on the nearby streets were dozens of "shteibels," one-room synagogues, organized by immigrants from a particular town, where men gathered to pray and share information.

Hester Street near Ludlow was home to "The Chazer Markt," the 'pig market' where everything but pig was for sale: fruits and vegetables, old coats, used eyeglasses, fish, bread, and hundreds of other items. "Hester Street was the pushcart center of the East Side," remembered novelist Anzia Yezierska. "The air reeked with the smell of fish and overripe fruit."

The bursting streets played multiple functions—workplace, marketplace, gathering place, playground: "Excitement, dirt, fighting, chaos! The sound of my street lifted like the blast of a great carnival or catastrophe. The noise was always in my ears. Even in sleep I could hear it; I can hear it now," wrote Michael Gold in his 1930 autobiographical novel, *Jews Without Money.*

(Above) Buying underwear from an Orchard Street pushcart. Photo by Browning, mid-1920s.
(Opposite) *Allen Street* by George Luks, 1905. Nearly every square inch of street was made use of on the Lower East Side.

The poverty here was real and painful. Garment industry work in particular was irregular, pay was low, and competition was fierce. For those with little or no money, there was not much sympathy, and pity was not easy to come by. Evictions were a recurring reality for many: "The Angel of Death, I thought, my landlady had come to put me out!" recalled Anzia Yezierska. "And Hester Street had gathered to watch another eviction." One journalist estimated the number of annual evictions on the Lower East Side in the 1890s at 30,000.

Overlooked within the Yiddish-speaking hubbub of the Jewish East Side was the small Sephardic or Levantine Jewish community. Arriving in the early 1900s and living within the Romanian colony around Chrystie, Forsyth, and Allen Streets, these Turkish, Greek, Balkan, and Syrian Jews brought their native lands' customs, language, cuisine, and world view. Accustomed to Mediterranean landscapes, Levantines found the New York environment shocking: "We live . . . in an oven of fire, in the midst of dirt and filth . . . in dark and narrow dwellings that inspire disgust," wrote Jack Farhi, a Bulgarian Jew, in the summer of 1912.

Indeed, the grim, overwhelming aspects of the East Side made its residents eager to escape as soon as they could to a quieter, more middle-class environment. In the early 1900s, they were aided by the opening of the Manhattan and Williamsburg Bridges and the new subway, which made it possible to work in Manhattan but live in a less frantic neighborhood. An exodus began to Brooklyn, the Bronx, and upper Manhattan.

But moving away didn't mean staying away. The theaters, food shops, restaurants, clothing and religious-article stores remained and drew visitors for decades. And something else brought them back: the Lower East Side had become "an American Jewish sacred space," in the phrase of historian Hasia Diner, and many just wanted to walk its streets and evoke the intense world that had once been here.

UPTOWN JEWS: RICH ON FIFTH AVENUE

At the same time that 350,000 Jews were crammed into the bursting Lower East Side, other "Israelites" were living a life of luxury. Only six miles north of Hester Street, Fifth Avenue had, by the

(Opposite top) Otto Kahn, a partner in Kuhn, Loeb, and Co., was a great patron of the Metropolitan Opera, c. 1912.
(Opposite bottom) Addie Wolff Kahn, wife of financier Otto Kahn, c. 1912.

(Above) Opulent home of Otto and Addie Wolff Kahn at 91st Street and Fifth Avenue, 1934. Their vast palazzo was opposite Andrew Carnegie's mansion.

1890s, become a neighborhood of the fabulously wealthy, and New York's German Jewish families were among them.

The Warburgs, Kahns, Lehmanns, Guggenheims, Schiffs, Seligmans, Strauses, and Bloomingdales had made their money in the garment trade, financial world, department stores, cigar business, and shipping industry. With their wealth, they built lavish homes close to those of America's superrich, such as Carnegie and Frick.

Otto Hermann Kahn's magnificent four-story mansion on 91st Street was complete with a ballroom that fit 250 guests, while Felix Warburg's home on 92nd Street was in the style of a French château. Other grand Jewish homes dotted the neighborhood, and years later Mrs. Warburg donated her mansion to be the home of New York's Jewish Museum, now a world-class institution.

WHEN HARLEM WAS JEWISH

North of the Fifth Avenue Jews, a Jewish community thrived in Harlem. From the 1880s through the 1910s, it bustled with synagogues, public baths, and a substantial Jewish population in which German Jews predominated. In 1887, one Harlem family, the Frankels of East 117 Street, proudly sent out engraved invitations to the confirmation (in Hebrew, "Bar Mitzvah") of their son Philip at Congregation B'nai Sholom on Lexington Avenue. Mr. and Mrs. Frankel, who were married in 1873 on Division Street in what was then Kleindeutschland, were still in Harlem in 1923 to celebrate their 50th wedding anniversary.

By the 1900s, Eastern Europeans and some Turkish and Greek Jews arrived in Harlem. By then, where you lived and prayed in Harlem revealed your economic status. Working-class Jews settled east of Sixth Avenue and built modest shuls in con-

---

(Above) In July, 1887, the Frankel family of Harlem celebrated the bar mitzvah of their eldest son, Philip, at Congregation B'nai Sholom.

verted brownstones. Affluent Germans lived and built their imposing synagogues—Ansche Chesed, Temple Israel, Shaare Zedek—in Central Harlem.

For a short time, Harlem was the third largest Jewish community in the world after the Lower East Side and Warsaw, Poland, with a Jewish population of well over 100,000. But in the 1920s, as the African-American population grew, Jewish congregations left their synagogues and Harlem's Jewish community waned. Several of those German congregations went on to reestablish themselves on the Upper West Side of Manhattan.

THE UPPER WEST SIDE

Somewhere between the rich Jews of the Upper East Side and the working and middle-class Jews of Harlem came the Jewish community of Manhattan's Upper West Side. By 1930, about 50,000 Jews already lived in the neighborhood between Broadway and the Hudson River, 79th to 110th Streets. Many were Eastern European entrepreneurs who had done well and were attracted to the convenience of the subway line that could take them directly to their businesses in the Garment District.

This neighborhood also drew many affluent Orthodox Jews who established synagogues in the area, including Young Israel, West Side Institutional, and The Jewish Center on West 86th Street. In the 1930s, a few thousand refugees from Hitler's Germany landed on the West Side. Jewish resettlement agencies initially housed them in West Side hotels such as the Millburn and the Marseilles, but these new arrivals eventually found their way to permanent apartments in the area.

FRANKFURT ON THE HUDSON

The most common landing place for the all-too-few escapees from Germany in the late 1930s was Washington Heights in

(Above) Bar mitzvah boy Philip Frankel in a typical photograph of the times.

upper Manhattan. Less expensive and less developed than the Upper West Side, Washington Heights was a refuge for so many German Jews that it earned the nicknames "The Fourth Reich" and "Frankfurt on the Hudson."

These refugees filled the neighborhood with the modern German language and culture, the vestiges of a nation that had murdered millions of their coreligionists and many of their relatives. From this area came numerous well-known American Jews, including New York Times editor Max Frankel, sex therapist and author Dr. Ruth Westheimer, and Secretary of State Henry Kissinger.

Jewish migration to New York City continued well into the latter part of the twentieth century. The Upper West Side, which began to fade as a Jewish community in the 1960s, began a resurgence during the 1980s and 1990s. In many respects the spirit of

Jewish migration lives on the Upper West Side, with several of New York City's oldest congregations found in the area, all of them having moved numerous times from their original downtown locations. They include Shearith Israel (1654), B'nai Jeshurun (1825), and Rodeph Sholom (1842).

The Upper West Side was not the only Jewish neighborhood to see a revival at the end of the twentieth century. The Lower East Side—most recently host to waves of Chinese and Latino immigrants—has been welcoming back a small number of young Jewish families. New residents found good company alongside art galleries and chic shops, and—in a turn of events that would surely have astonished its early twentieth-century inhabitants—the community became certifiably "hip."

(Above) Upper West Side Shul: Rabbi Jacob Meir Sagalowitch stands in front of the synagogue he founded on West 79 Street during World War II. His wife, Bluma, and grandson Joel Sagall are shown beside him.

(Above) View of Williamsburg, Brooklyn, 1972. An important Jewish neighborhood since the early 1900s, Williamsburg today is home to many Satmar Hasidim. Photograph by Nathan Benn.

Chapter Three

GOTTA EARN A DOLLAR:

How They Made a Living

New York City has for several centuries offered a promise to the destitute and downtrodden of the world: venture here and you too can struggle to earn a living in our highly competitive, intensely commercial metropolis. Millions of Jews took that challenge, found success, and along the way attempted almost every occupation imaginable.

By the middle of the twentieth century, New York City was overflowing with Jewish cab drivers, doctors, shopkeepers, lawyers, waiters, teachers, bakers, accountants, salesmen, printers, and restaurateurs. The Big Apple has also drawn many Jews into the television, magazine, newspa-

per, book publishing, and internet businesses. And some professions—such as diamond dealing and psychiatry—have long been mainstays of the Jewish New York working world.

New York Jews have always had a special relationship with the public school system. From the 1950s on, nearly half of the city's teachers were Jewish, as was an even higher percentage of the principals. On the high holy days of Rosh Hashanah and Yom Kippur, the schools were virtual ghost towns because of absent Jewish students, faculty, and administration. Finally, in 1960, the city decided to close the schools on those days for everyone.

(Above) Snuff and tobacco for sale, in Yiddish and English, on Division Street in a 1938 Berenice Abbott photograph.
(Opposite) Abraham and Straus department store delivery wagons, late 1890s.

JULIUS "Yoile" OKUN
HEBREW HEAVYWEIGHT CHAMPIONSHIP
CONTENDER
Charlie Johnston, *Manager*
1465 Broadway, New York City

In New York City, Jews took jobs that had never before been associated with Jewry. Police Commissioner Theodore Roosevelt encouraged "fighting Jews" in the 1890s to join his department—and, eventually, the city had hundreds of Jewish police officers. To this day, Jewish cops have their own fraternal organization, the Shomrim Society, and New York's firefighters the Ner Tamid, the Brotherhood of Jewish Firefighters.

The tough turf of the Lower East Side brought forth a number of world-champion Jewish boxers. Probably the most famous was Benjamin Leiner, who boxed under the name "Benny Leonard." Leonard, who often wore a Star of David on his boxing shorts, was world lightweight champion from 1917 through 1924, when he finally retired from the ring. Other notable New York prizefighters included Maxie Rosebloom (light heavyweight champion,

(Left) A job for a nice Jewish boy? Hebrew Heavyweight Contender Julius "Yoile" Okun. (Right) Collectible card for World Lightweight Champion Benny Leonard.

34

1930-34), Charley Rosenberg (world bantamweight champion, 1925-27), and Abe Goldstein (bantamweight champion, 1924).

STOCKBROKERS IN LITTLE OLDE NEW YORK

On the more genteel side of things, Jewish stockbrokers had been in business since at least 1792, when at least four of the twenty-four founders of the New York Stockbrokers Guild (later renamed the New York Stock Exchange) were Jewish, including Ephraim Hart, Isaac Gomez, Alexander Zuntz, and Benjamin Seixas.

A small number of educated Jews with German roots found investment banking a fertile field. Abraham Kuhn, Solomon Loeb, Jacob Schiff, Joseph and Jesse Seligman, Felix Warburg, Otto Kahn, and Marcus Goldman and his son-in-law Samuel Sachs founded or built influential firms, such as Kuhn Loeb, Goldman Sachs, and Shearson Lehman. The New York–based J & W Seligman & Co. bankrolled the Union Army during the Civil War, selling more than $200 million in bonds through the German branch of their business.

German-Jewish men generally arrived in the United States with little capital or education. Many began by peddling—selling goods door to door with a pack on their back, or in an on-the-street pushcart. That demanding work frequently led to grander things. Two brothers, Oscar and Isidor Straus, built on the modest crockery business their father had started, eventually bought two struggling businesses and turned them into the major retail stores Abraham and Straus and R. H. Macy's. The Bloomingdale Brothers started small, but by the 1870s, they had opened their enormous department store

(Right) An 1887 advertisement shows Bloomingdale's, already an enormous department store.

BLOOMINGDALE

THIRD AVENUE, —— 59th &

THE POPULARITY and this establishment is n fact that our prices are the low recognize that our goods are th in every respect, and that eve is made to serve them accepta

Our store, while it is one without doubt the best equi of New York. Yet one s proven that even this mam not large enough to meet of our growing trade. An a to Sixtieth Street has rec menced and will be pushe as possible. When complete

(Above) Employees working hard at Moe Levy & Co.'s garment factory in 1911. Photograph by Joseph Byron.

on Lexington Avenue. Other German-Jewish New Yorkers built grand emporiums such as B. Altman's, Stern's, and May's.

THE SAGA OF THE SHMATA BUSINESS

The clothing trade had a very powerful impact on the business fortunes and fates of Jewish New Yorkers. At one point in the early twentieth century, six out of ten New York Jews who were employed were involved in the production of clothing.

The garment industry's vocabulary was familiar to all of Jewish New York—piecework, sweatshops, child labor, conflict between German Jewish bosses and Eastern European employees, union organizing struggles, bitter strikes. The industry was at the heart of one of the worst New York tragedies of the twentieth century: the death of over 140 young women, more than half of them Jewish, in the Triangle Shirtwaist Company fire of 1911.

German Jews had settled in New York at the perfect moment to enter the garment business. Until the mid-1800s, most American families produced their own clothes or bought custom-made outfits. During the 1830s, used clothing was a saleable commodity. When the sewing machine made the mass production of new garments possible in the 1840s and '50s, used clothes merchants moved over to manufacturing. By 1880, the garment business was New York's biggest industry and garment workers were producing the largest percentage of America's manufactured clothing. German-born Jews had a virtual monopoly. By that time they owned eighty percent of all retail and ninety percent of all wholesale clothing firms in the city.

At just that moment, of course, the tidal wave of Eastern European Jews began arriving in New York City. To affluent German professionals living comfortably uptown, these exotic, impoverished, pious or socialistic,

(Above) Rose Schneiderman, a Polish immigrant to the Lower East Side, rose from the ranks of garment workers to become a leading union organizer.
(Following spread left) Jewish workers in a millinery (hat-making) factory, c. 1920. (Following spread right) Printers working for the *Forverts*.

unassimilated Yiddish-speaking crowds were deeply unsettling. The assimilated Jews worried—not without reason—that the massive arrival of their Eastern European coreligionists might adversely affect their standing with their non-Jewish neighbors.

But to the clothing manufacturer, these Eastern Europeans were a source of cheap labor—a "czar-sent opportunity," in the words of historians Edwin Burrow and Mike Wallace. By the turn of the twentieth century, over 150,000 Jews were working in the garment industry, many for German-Jewish bosses, as tailors, cap makers, cloak makers, furriers, milliners, pressers, sewing-machine operators, and shirtwaist (blouse) makers. The work was seasonal, hours were long, pay was low, and working conditions were awful.

LABOR PAINS, UNION STRUGGLES

There had been confrontations between Jewish employers and employees in New York since the 1870s, but these often bitter battles were small scale and difficult for workers to win. Starting in 1909, however, several massive general strikes occurred, linking

workers across New York. Jewish women led the way that November, when 20,000 women walked out across the city's shirtwaist and skirt industry. Their strike ended with minimal gains, but citywide sympathy and growing public support promised better outcomes ahead.

In 1910, 60,000 cloakmakers walked out in the largest strike in New York City history up to that point. Physical assaults on picketing strikers and bitter verbal attacks made this overwhelmingly Jewish conflict deeply alarming to the affluent "uptown" Jews. Community leaders Jacob Schiff and Louis Marshall, seeking a breakthrough solution, called in Boston lawyer Louis Brandeis. Brandeis's mediation led to an agreement known as "the protocol of peace," which set new standards for the treatment of workers and brought the strike to an end.

Jewish labor struggles continued throughout the twentieth century. After more than half a century on the Lower East Side, the garment industry moved uptown in the 1930s to the area just south of Times Square. By the 1970s, the industry's unions no longer had many Jewish members; they had retired, and their children had gone on to other professions. New immigrants and other New York ethnic groups took their place. There were still labor struggles to be fought, but the new workers were clearly the beneficiaries of many of the hard-won battles of earlier days when the industry was dominated by Jews.

The New York garment industry was smaller in size and influence at the end of the twentieth century than it was at the beginning of the nineteen hundreds. The more prominent Jewish contemporary clothing designers and entrepreneurs include Calvin Klein, Ralph Lauren, Donna Karan, Anne Klein, Eileen Fisher, and Arnold Scaasi, among others.

And today, appropriately, on Seventh Avenue and 38th Street, a larger-than-life-size statue of a Jewish man at his sewing machine bears witness to the Jewish legacy in the garment industry's labor struggles.

**(Above) Louis D. Brandeis brokered the "Protocol of Peace" between New York Jewish unions and owners in 1910. Seen here in a 1930s photo by Jessie Tarbox Beals.
(Right) A strike by the Hebrew Butcher Workers Union, 1930s. Photograph by Herbert Sonnenfeld.**

Chapter Four
CAFES, KNISHES, AND CHALLAH:
The Joys of New York's Jewish Food

Jewish New York reveled, and was revealed, in its food. Like much of American Jewish culture, Jewish food was a hybrid—a mishmash of old-world cooking and customs, Jewish dietary laws, and an ongoing accommodation with American life.

The concentration of Jews on the Lower East Side meant many mouths hungry for the wares of Jewish food sellers. For years, pushcarts and peddlers lined the packed streets selling herring and smoked fish, pickles and roast potatoes, challah and halvah. A survey of pushcarts in 1906 found 2,362 peddlers in the district south of 14th Street and east of Broadway. Eventually, the pushcarts were pushed out by city regulators and replaced by the Essex Street indoor market.

What New York Jews ate was a function of custom and kashruth. Jewish dietary law was kept by some and violated by many. Eventually, "kosher-style"—an American invention—became as popular, if not more, than kosher itself. But kosher food kept its place: by 1934 New York had about 12,000 kosher food processors and dealers, with combined annual sales above $200 million.

Still, it was probably custom as much as religious devotion that kept kosher chicken markets and butchers busy. Contentiousness was always on the menu for a poor population, as evidenced by the 1902 demonstrations led by east side

(Above) Beinish Dienstag's kosher knishes could be had for a nickel on the city streets in 1933.
(Opposite) Exterior view of Nathan's Hot Dog Emporium at Coney Island, August 1954.

women against the rising prices of kosher meat and bread. The protests were called "The War of the Women against the Butchers," and ended in a citywide victory.

A sampling of the 631 food dealers doing business in the center of the East Side Tenth Ward in 1899 included 140 groceries, 131 butcher shops, 36 bakeries, 14 butter and egg stores, 62 candy stores, 21 fruit stands, and 10 delicatessens. Money may have been scarce for many Eastsiders, but there was never a paucity of available food.

At the end of the first decade of the twentieth century, the Lower East Side boasted more than sixty delicatessens featuring Eastern European Jewish food. In the cafés—"Jewish saloons," as one wag called them—journalists, union men, workers, artists, and anyone else looking for an escape could argue and kibitz, debate, and discuss the day's events "over steaming Russian tea and lemon, thin slices of cake, and Russian cigarettes."

By 1905, some 250 to 300 coffeehouses were operating on the Lower East Side. In addition to the less formal eating establishments in the area, more "fashionable restaurants" appeared on its frantic streets. Over the years, they included:

- Café Royale, Second Avenue at 12th Street (called "the Sardi's of the Yiddish actors, the Algonquin of the Yiddish writers")
- Odessa Private Restaurant, 42 Essex Street
- Leiber Grill, Bucovina Private Restaurant, 116 Essex Street
- Seifs, 15 East Houston Street
- H Harris Delicatessen and Lunch Room, 468 Grand Street
- Shoilem Tumases Rumanian Wine Tavern, 154 Allen Street
- Morris Dorff Russian Tea Café and Restaurant, 70 Eldridge Street
- Oxford Café, 211 Bowery
- Vienna Restaurant, 175 East Houston Street

(Above) Hand-painted fowl were a familiar sight on Lower East Side butcher shop windows. Photograph by Andreas Feininger, 1940.
(Opposite left) M. Bloom—a typical Jewish delicatessen with proprietor and family posing in the doorway.

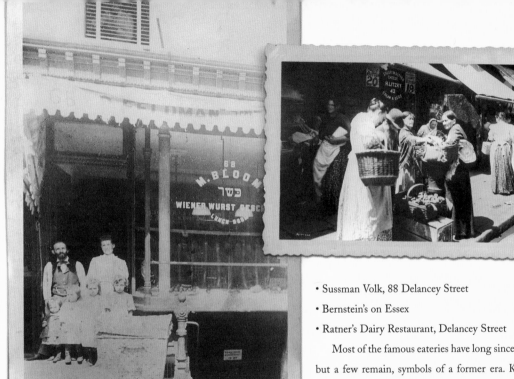

- Sussman Volk, 88 Delancey Street
- Bernstein's on Essex
- Ratner's Dairy Restaurant, Delancey Street

Most of the famous eateries have long since closed their doors, but a few remain, symbols of a former era. Katz's Delicatessen, where the World War II era slogan, "Send a Salami to Your Boy in the Army" originated, has been on the Lower East Side since

(Above right) Shoppers examine curbside wares in front of H. Litzky's food store, c. 1898. Photograph by the Byron Studio. (Following spread left) Picture postcard of "A Pickle Vendor in the Ghetto, New York City," c. 1912. (Following spread right) "A Jewish store, Jewish Quarter," in an early twentieth-century postcard.

A Pickle Vender in the Ghetto,
New York City

M. OLTARSH
14
HARDWARE
TOOLS & CUTLERY

POST CARD

This side for Correspondence. | This side for Address.

TRENTON
JUL
4 PM
1912

2 Cents

U. S. Series 10

488-18

jewish store, Jewish quarter, New York.

LOU G. SIEGEL, INC., 209 WEST 38TH STREET, NEW YORK 18, N. Y.

(Above) Lou G. Siegel's Garment-Center Grill billed itself as "America's Foremost Kosher Restaurant."

1888. Yonah Schimmel's famous knishery, not far away on Houston Street, began doing business in 1910.

For more than four decades, the Garden Cafeteria on Essex and East Broadway was a gathering place for Jewish writers, artists, actors, and agitators. "Many intellectual leaders come into the cafes to pour out wisdom and drink tea," reported one observer in the 1920s. That era faded in the 1950s and the Garden closed in 1983. But a newer eat-and-kibitz place, the Second Avenue Deli in the northern boundary of the Lower East Side (East 10th Street), opened in 1954.

THE SEPHARDIM ATE, TOO

Sephardic Jews, though far smaller in number on the East Side, had their own gathering places. Levantine cafés, restaurants, and grocery stores sprang up between 1900 and the 1930s. The strictly kosher, Syrian-style Egyptian Rose's restaurant, for example, served a regular Levantine clientele, particularly single men. Located in the heart of the Sephardic district on the corner of Allen and Grand Streets, it was opened in 1919 by Rose Cohen Misrie and her husband, Israel, and remained in business until 1949. The clientele was predominantly Syrian, Greek, and Turkish Jews.

Egyptian Rose wasn't Egyptian; Rose's family was Syrian, and she immigrated to the United States from Tripoli, Libya, in 1906, at the age of eight. Her cooking reflected her Syrian heritage: mahshi (vegetables stuffed with rice and meat), and meat pies, kibbe, and kofte. Mondays and Thursdays at Egyptian Rose were Dairy Days, and Mrs. Misrie served yogurt, rice with lentils, and sabbusak (pastries filled with kashkeval cheese).

(Above) Isadore Pinkowitz started his business producing kosher frankfurters in New York. His company grew into Hebrew National.

Coffeehouses were multipurpose establishments for Sephardim as well as for Ashkenazim. The patrons gossiped, sought employment, played backgammon, and debated the day's hot topics. In the 1930s, they could visit Jo Levy's Turkish Jewish nightclub on Allen Street, where Middle Eastern music and dancing came with the menu.

FOOD STORES GALORE

Stores that catered to Eastern European Jewish tastes flourished on the Lower East Side—and beyond—even after the East Side ceased to be home to most Jews. By one account, as late as the mid-1930s, a visitor could find thirty-six different appetizing

stores on the East Side. By that time, numerous businesses that began on the Lower East Side had moved uptown or out into the larger arena of New York City's boroughs.

In Manhattan's Garment District (the West 30s), Jewish workers and bosses were fed by a colony of mostly kosher restaurants, among them S&H's Dairy Kosher Vegetarian Restaurant; Dubrow's Cafeteria; Felix's Kosher Dining Room; Garfein's Kosher Family Restaurant; and the Vitamine Vegetarian and Dairy Restaurant. The elegant Lou G. Siegel on West 38th Street

called itself "America's Foremost Kosher restaurant." Part of the fame of Trotzky's Kosher Restaurant on West 35th Street came from the fact that, recalled one observer, "the waiters were notoriously rude," a trait that became a trademark of a number of Jewish restaurants.

(Left) Still famous today, Katz's has been welcoming customers for decades. Photograph by Richard Berenholtz. (Above) They can still "send a salami" at Katz's kosher-style deli. Photograph of general manager Dave Tarowsky by Harvey Wang, 1995.

81st Street, and on West 72nd Street, another dairy restaurant called itself "Famous" and attracted clientele that included Isaac Bashevis Singer. The Upper West Side was, and still is, home to such appetizing food stores as Barney Greengrass and the world-renowned Zabar's.

Some, however, stayed nearer to where they began. Galician immigrant Joel Russ sold herring on the street—first from a horse-and-wagon and later on a pushcart—and by 1914, Russ had opened his own store on Orchard Street. Because his pretty daughters were working with him, he called the store Russ and Daughters when it moved to Houston Street. Russ's grandson Mark Federman took over the smoked fish emporium and tried to keep faithful to the "old style."

The Upper West Side of Manhattan, where affluent Jews had moved, now boasted numerous places for kosher and kosher-style dining. Fine and Schapiro, a kosher restaurant, opened in 1927. Steinberg's Dairy Restaurant was famous on Broadway and

(Above left) Natalie Spatz holds Ratner's famous onion rolls. After nearly ninety years of serving the Lower East Side, Ratner's closed in 2002. Photograph by Harvey Wang, 1989. (Above middle) Mark Russ Federman, third-generation owner of Russ and Daughters appetizing store on Houston Street. Photograph by Harvey Wang, 1993. (Above right) Louis and Lillian Zabar opened an appetizing counter in a Manhattan supermarket in 1934. Today, it is the world famous Jewish culinary landmark—Zabar's. Photograph by Richard Berenholtz.

Federman notes one exception to his grandfather's era: "I did get my own counter people, who are nice to the customers."

FOOD AND WINE FOR THE MASSES

As the Jewish community grew larger, so too did the demand for retail products available from Jewish entrepreneurs. The Lower East Side became a launching pad for numerous companies: Isaac Gellis kosher meats, Hebrew National Delicatessen, Goodman's Noodles, Barton's Kosher Candy, Rokeach foods. Partly because they emanated from the American center of Jewish authenticity, these products succeeded on a national level.

In their heyday, Jewish bakeries produced huge numbers of bagels and bialys. Matzoh, of course, was an urgent, annual need for the Jewish population during the Passover season and required special attention. Matzoh makers had been in operation on the Lower East Side as early as the 1830s, and by 1910 five matzoh factories were located in the area. They included Horowitz Brothers and Margareten, which had factories on East 4th Street, Meyer London's Matzos Bakery on Bayard Street, and the Finesilver Matzoh Baking Company on Pitt Street. The Horowitz and Margareten Matzoh story was especially poignant: the family started with a grocery store on Willet Street in 1883, producing matzoh first for their own use, then later for customers, too. The business grew even after Regina Margareten's mother, father, and husband died. Despite the losses in the family, Regina grew the business steadily over the next forty years.

Carbonated water is another Jewish gustatory success story. In 1880, two seltzer producers opened on the East Side. Twenty-

(Above left) The labels of New York's kosher wineries featured Jewish stars, holy-land views, and even the tablets of the Ten Commandments.
(Above right) Schapiro's famous New York State Honey Wine, specially sweetened.

seven years later, thanks to the exploding immigrant population and its thirst, more than a hundred companies were manufacturing "East Side champagne."

Then there is the tale of Schapiro wines. Sam Schapiro immigrated to the United States and began making wine on the Lower East Side in 1899. Sam proudly proclaimed his wine was "so thick you can cut it with a knife." It may not have been a gourmet boast, but it worked for the company, which operated a wine cellar on Rivington Street until 2001. (Somewhere along the way, "almost" entered the slogan, as in "almost cut with a knife." It is doubtful, however, that the wine got much thinner.)

Today, kosher food is a multibillion dollar business. The bialy from Bialystock has made its presence known in cities around the United States and the little Jewish bagel has emerged from New York City and conquered the world.

(Above left) This rabbi was hired to supervise the production of kosher wines in a Lower East Side wine cellar. Photograph by Marjory Collins, 1942.

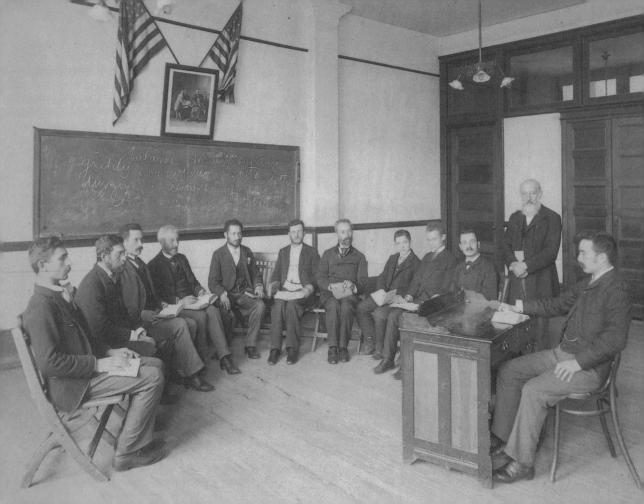

Chapter Five
MOVING UP:
Learning and Giving

"It is enough that I am a merchant,' said a long-gabardined peddler yesterday. 'What is such a life? What can I do for my people or myself? My boy shall be a lawyer, learned and respected of men. And it is for that that I stand here, sometimes when my feet ache so that I would gladly go and rest. My boy shall have knowledge. He shall go to college.'

"College! That is the aim and ambition of hundreds of them.... The father ... dreams of a better life than his own for the boy or girl who is so dear to his heart. When the evening comes and the day's work is over, he sits in the little tenement ... and instills into his children's minds the necessity for knowledge."

—"EAST SIDE LOVE OF LEARNING,"
NEW YORK TRIBUNE, SEPTEMBER 18, 1898

The word "Jewish" does not appear anywhere in the above excerpt from a *New York Tribune* article, but few readers would miss its implied presence. This immigrant, like so many others, brought to New York two powerful Jewish values: a love of learning and the obligation to contribute to the welfare of the larger community (in Hebrew, "tzedakah").

These attributes played a crucial role in the rise of Jewish New York. Without their passion for learning, many Jewish New Yorkers would have lacked the tools to succeed. And without the organizations that the Jewish community created to support its members, their journey would have been far more difficult.

(Above) Yeshiva University in Washington Heights: A great center of Jewish learning in the city.
(Opposite) Adult Education courses at the Educational Alliance, such as this English class, were frequently offered at night.

NEW LEARNING IN THE NEW WORLD

Learning was an old-world Jewish tradition, but it took a different form in New York. For one thing, literacy was far more valuable in this urban setting than it had been in small-town Eastern Europe. For another, here the educational impulse turned toward secular learning, something generally not available to Jews in the Russian Empire.

New York City public schools were free and open to all. But, as Lillian Wald of the Henry Street Settlement observed, east-side schools were incredibly crowded, with classes that had "as many as sixty pupils in a single room, and often three children on a seat." At the high-water mark of Jewish immigration, an army hospital ship had to be converted into a school and moored on the East River. From 1905 through 1910, approximately 10,000 Lower East Side children took classes on board.

The overcrowding was partly a result of Jewish families' great desire to send their children to school. Despite these feelings, however, in the early 1900s many Russian Jewish children dropped out before high school because their families needed the extra income that a youngster's labor provided. As the years wore on, hard-working, bright, ambitious Jewish students filled the city's high schools, including elite institutions such as Townsend Harris and Stuyvesant High School. After their secondary education was completed, many went on to the New York's city colleges: College of the City of New York (CCNY) for men and Hunter College for women.

CCNY had been founded in 1847 as a no-cost academy for the bright sons of New York and by the late 1800s, a large percentage of students were German Jews. "At least 500 of the 1677 students at the New York City College, where

(Above) One distinguished graduate of the Educational Alliance Art School paints a portrait of another: Moses Soyer captures sculptor Chaim Gross on canvas.

tuition and books are free, are Jewish boys from the East Side," wrote Abraham Cahan in 1898 in an article in *Atlantic Monthly*. A dozen years later in 1910, 90 of the 112 graduating students were Jewish, most of them from Eastern-European families. For many years thereafter, the percentage of Jewish students was extraordinarily high at CCNY (which led smart-alecks to decode its acronym as the "Circumcised Citizens of New York"). At Hunter College, also, by the 1920s Jewish women had become a disproportionate percentage of the attendees.

Jewish interest in higher education was driven by the dual desires to further oneself academically as well as economically. Dr. S. Josephine Baker, a New York City health-care official around the turn of the century, remarked on how families viewed their children's education as an investment: "While [their son] was being educated [at law or medical school], the whole family worked like mad under sweat-shop conditions and skimped incredibly on food, clothes, and rent, not to mention soap and sunlight. Then when the chosen son started making money, they moved out and followed his rising fortunes uptown; first to Lexington Avenue . . . then to Riverside Drive. And sometimes finally to Park Avenue."

In fact, thousands of Jewish boys, fulfilling their families' expectations, did go on to college and became professionals. Thousands of others did not take the college route, but still became successful businessmen, shopkeepers, and entrepreneurs.

AN ALLIANCE FOR EDUCATION

The institution that perhaps best exemplified the combining of tzedakah and learning was the Educational Alliance, housed in a five-story building at 197 East Broadway just off Straus Square. From the moment it began operating, the Alliance aimed to assist Eastern European Jews to succeed in America. Supported by the philanthropy of German Jews such as Isidor Straus and Jacob Schiff, the Alliance was created from the affiliation of three other Jewish organizations. It offered health-care, child-care, physical activities, social work, and legal counsel to

(Following spread left) Americanization Day: 500 or more children attended these exercises in waving the flag—and pledging allegiance to it—at the Educational Alliance.
(Following spread right) Preparing poor immigrant children for public school, prior to 1914. These courses were often paid for by the Baron de Hirsch fund.

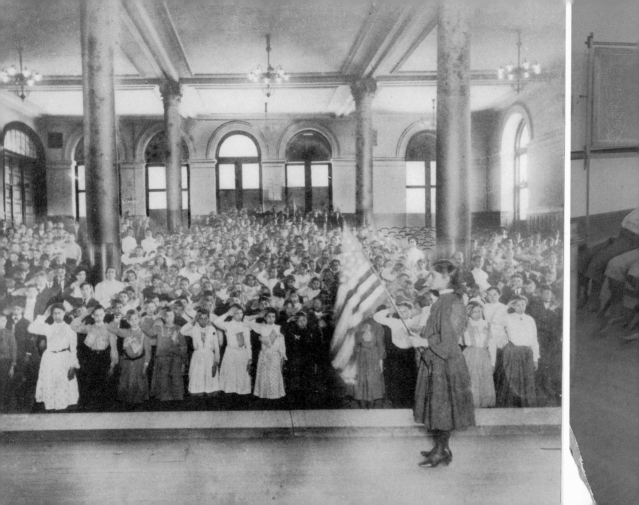

the inhabitants of poor urban neighborhoods, and it promoted—as its name promised—education.

The Alliance offered residents of the Lower East Side a wide menu of enrichment: lectures, day and night instruction in the English language, and "Americanization," a reading room and library, classes in cooking, sewing, music, theater, and art. Art lessons cost three cents and were attended by many future artists: painters Moses and Isaac Soyer, Mark Rothko, Barnett Newman, Ben Shahn, Leonard Baskin, and Abraham Walkowitz; and sculptors Jacob Epstein, Chaim Gross, and Jo Davidson. Other Alliance students included comedian Eddie Cantor, influential CCNY philosophy professor Morris Raphael Cohen, and broadcasting executive David Sarnoff.

Despite all the good that it did, the Alliance had a mixed reception by its recipients. The institution's German Jewish bene-factors "poured money, time, and energy into the Alliance, and often were rewarded by the downtown Jews with fury and scorn," wrote historian Irving Howe. The immigrants were highly sensitive to condescension, and the uptown Jews were certainly guilty of it on numerous occasions. Despite the grumbling, however, the Alliance's superb offerings made a difference, and well into the beginning of the twenty-first century, it continues its service to the community out of the building on Straus Square.

TZEDAKAH AND TSOURIS

Conflict over tzedakah was not unfamiliar in Jewish New York. In every generation, Jewish philanthropic, fraternal, health, and relief organizations have worked to meet the community's needs. Administering those organizations, however, was sometimes complicated by the growing diversity of the Jewish population.

(Above) The Jewish Child Care Agency provided education even for the very young. The Hebrew Orphan Asylum in Upper Manhattan sheltered thousands of homeless youngsters from 1880 until it closed in 1941. Among its alumni: humor writer Art Buchwald.

(Above) For a consultation fee of 25 cents, the Alliance's Legal Aid Bureau helped with domestic and commercial grievances.
In 1925, the Bureau was consulted on nearly 5,000 cases.

In the old country, the Jewish communal board, or kehillah, had been the resource for needy Jews. But as Jews from different lands, with different forms of worship, arrived at New York's synagogues, a variety of misunderstandings, disagreements, and struggles for leadership ensued. The result, as early as the 1820s, was the creation of aid societies independent of the synagogue.

The first was the Hebrew Benevolent Society, founded in 1822 by leaders of Congregation Shearith Israel, who were mostly native-born members of English and Dutch ancestry. In 1844, the German Hebrew Benevolent Society was founded by—and offered aid to—only German Jews. This split persisted until 1859. In the intervening years, as New York City's Jewish population increased rapidly from 500 in 1820 to 60,000 in 1860, the community formed many aid and philanthropic groups: free loan associations, immigrant–aid societies, fuel benevolent organizations (to help the indigent buy winter fuel), and numerous others.

Eventually, Jewish New Yorkers united around the need for hospitals and an orphanage. Many were eager for an institution that would willingly tend to sick, needy, and aged Jews, and that would offer kosher food. The community also wanted to eliminate the problem of Christian clergymen visiting hospitalized Jews with the intent of converting them. In 1855, a "Jews' Hospital" opened on West 28th Street. In its earliest years, it admitted only Jews, except for emergency cases. By 1864, the hospital opened up to all faiths, treating a huge number of them for no charge. In 1866, the institution changed its name to Mount Sinai and is now internationally acknowledged as an exceptional medical institution.

In 1859, the benevolent societies finally joined forces. One of their first acts was the creation of a Hebrew Orphan Asylum, which opened that year. In 1874, that organization expanded again, absorbing four other groups and becoming United Hebrew Charities.

AIDING THE EASTERN EUROPEANS

When immigration rapidly increased in the 1880s, already-existing organizations attempted to help the new Russian immigrants. To meet demand, however, hundreds of new groups were created. By necessity, Eastern European Jews already here—with a keen sense of their fellow-immigrants' most pressing needs—launched many of the most influential and effective institutions themselves.

Among the most valuable Eastern European creations were "landsmanshaften," or self-help associations made up of immigrants from the same towns in Europe. These groups procured many important services for their members, including loans, burial plots, insurance policies, social meeting places, and much more. Over 500 landsmanshaften operated in New York by 1915, representing even the tiniest of Eastern European Jewish towns.

Another crucial organization built by Eastern European Jews was the Hebrew Immigrant Aid Society (HIAS), which began helping immigrants under another name in 1882. HIAS representatives met Jews on Ellis Island, helped them find relatives, avoid tricksters, find lodging, and secure jobs. HIAS produced multilingual guides for immigrants, represented them at hearings, and worked tirelessly as their advocates with the shipping lines and governments. To this day HIAS continues to serve Jews worldwide in matters of immigration and naturalization.

COORDINATING COMMUNITY-WIDE NEEDS

As the number of aid groups increased, it became obvious that there needed to be a centralized coordinating body to eliminate overlap and counterproductive competition for funds. In 1917, banker Felix Warburg brought together community leaders to found what became the Federation of Jewish Philanthropies. Seven decades later, Federation merged with another major tzedakah coordinating organization, the United Jewish Appeal.

UJA-Federation of New York today is an enormously sophisticated organization offering help to Jewish communities across the world and coordinating a network of local groups with a combined budget over $1 billion. In its mission, "To care for those in need, strengthen Jewish peoplehood, and foster Jewish renaissance in New York, in Israel, and throughout the world," it brings together the multiple strands of the long, proud history of New York Jewish tzedakah.

ICE TO THOMASHEFSKY'S ROUMANIAN VILLAGE, 181 ALLEN ST., NEW YORK CITY

Chapter Six:
FROM YIDDISH THEATER TO JEWISH-AMERICAN CULTURE

The Jewish cultural contribution to New York City has been nothing short of remarkable. Jewish writers, musicians, poets, playwrights, lyricists, composers, painters, sculptors, actors, directors, comics, and entertainers have greatly enriched the lively artistic scene for which New York is well known. In addition, Jewish patronage of the arts has played a major role in making the city's cultural tapestry one of the most vivid in the world.

The unprecedented outpouring of artistic talent truly began with the arrival of Eastern European Jews; the Sephardi and German Jews of earlier days produced few notable artists. One of the exceptions was Myer Myers, an eighteenth-century silversmith whose fine works rivaled those of Paul Revere. Journalist, playwright, and diplomat Mordecai Manuel Noah had some success on the New York stage in the early 1800s. And of course there was that nineteenth-century poet of mixed Sephardi–Ashkenazi parents whose early works attracted praise from Ralph Waldo Emerson and Ivan Turgenev; sadly, Emma Lazarus died before reaching age forty, and her most important poem, "The New Colossus," only became famous posthumously, despite its stirring lines, "Give me your tired, your poor, your huddled masses yearning to breathe free."

(Above) Artist Jacob Epstein sketched Jewish East Side café life, c. 1902.
(Opposite) Boris Thomashefsky's Roumanian Village Theater, 181 Allen Street, offered musical entertainment, drinks, and dancing.

New York's German Jewish community's passionate support of the arts extends as far back as the 1840s and '50s, when the Lower East Side was Kleindeutschland ("Little Germany"), populated by German Christians as well as Jews. Historian Stanley Nadel noted that "Anti-Semites who visited New York were shocked to discover that such bastions of German culture as New York City's German theaters were dependent on Jewish theatergoers."

IGNITING JEWISH CREATIVITY

The extraordinary Yiddish Theater scene and the dynamic Yiddish newspaper business of the late nineteenth and early twentieth centuries truly mark a peak of creativity in the cultural life of Jewish New York. The New York Yiddish Theater spoke powerfully to its audience, and, on occasion, the audience spoke back. The plays were operatic versions of Old Testament stories, slapstick comedies of "green-horn" antics (*The Rabbi's Family*), and heart-rending melodramas of the gulf between old-country and new-world Jews. Playwrights also borrowed plots from such theatrical luminaries as Ibsen, Gogol, and Shakespeare, twisting them into Jewish tales (*The Jewish King Lear* and *Mirele Efros, The Jewish Queen Lear*).

Theatergoing was an essential component of immigrant life. During the early 1900s, more than 1,000 performances a year were given before an audience of about two million paying customers. Four major Yiddish theaters—the Grand, the People's, the Thalia, and the Windsor—opened around the Bowery, each individually seating well over 1,000. The theaters were often full, despite tickets that cost twenty-five cents to a dollar at a time when many workers made less than ten dollars a week.

Theatrical leads such as Boris Thomashefsky, Jacob Adler, Molly Picon, and Bertha Kalich were stars of major magnitude and adored by fans throughout the world. Jacob Adler "had a court, and when you saw him in the streets he was preceded and

(Above) Molly Picon in costume for the musical *Abi Gezunt*. Called "the bean-sized Bernhardt" by *Variety*, Picon charmed audiences for over eighty years.

Boris Thomashefsky

באָריס טאָמאַשעפּסקי

THE ENSEMBLE OF THOMASHEFSKY'S ROUMANIAN VILLAGE, 181 ALLEN ST., NEW YORK CITY

PHOTO-GLOSS

POST CARD Robert D. Shapiro
Presents

Exclusive Atmosphere at
Thomashefsky's Roumanian Village
181 ALLEN STREET   NEW YORK CITY
PHONE, DRYDOCK 4-8964
NIGHTLY REVIEWS
PRESENTING AN ALL STAR CAST
FEATURING
BORIS THOMASHEFSKY
AND REGINA ZUCKERBERG
BAR AND DANCING
ENTERTAINMENT NEVER STOPS

BORIS THOMASHEFSKY,
REGINA ZUCKERBERG
and Company.

באָריס טאָמאַשעפּסקי,
רעגינא צוקערבערג
אין קאַמפּאַני, דירעקטאָר פֿון ניו יאָרק
בלויז פֿאַר 1 אָוװענד
אין זייער גרויסען סוקסעס
"דאָס ציגיינער ליעד"
"THE GYPSY SONG"

followed by his fans," recalled Jacob Epstein, a Jewish artist who grew up on the Lower East Side.

What made the theater so significant and popular? Part of the answer lies in the lives of the patrons. Their days were filled with dramatic struggle, social dislocation, clashes between family members over new- and old-world values, and tremendous economic pressures. In an era before radio or TV, when film was in its infancy, buying a ticket to a show offered these uprooted people a way to see their stories and dilemmas portrayed dramatically and publicly. As a result, fevered emotion filled the seats as well as the stage, with audiences often offering comments directly on the action. Sometimes, actors would respond, tossing asides of their own back at the eager patrons.

Thomashefksy's performances were legendary for their emotional resonance. One theatergoer recalled, "When he sang 'A Briv-

(Above) Boris Thomashefsky (seated at right) was not only the Yiddish theater's master of melodrama. He also ran his own theater and assembled an acting ensemble.

PEOPLES THE TRE

BOWERY & SPRING ST.
SCHULMAN & ROVENGE MGR.

TEL. ORCHARD 0478
MAX ROSENTHAL DIRECTOR

– NOW PLAYING –

עם צדיק'ס משפחה

SAMUEL GOLDENBERG – LUDWIG SATZ
BERTHA GERSTEN – NETTIE TOBIAS

IN A SCENE FROM

THE RABBI'S FAMILY"

WITH AN ALL STAR CAST

See Ludwig SATZ

in his masterful creation

J. RUMSHINSKY'S

SENSATIONAL
THRILLING

NOW!
PLAYING

STUPENDOUS
MUSICAL
PRODUCTION

Enchanting
MUSIC

"MOSHIACH KUMT"

משיח
קומט

Libretto by
WM. SIEGEL

Directed by
Ludwig SATZ

SATZ
PUBLIC THEATRE
RUMSHINSKY

66-SECOND AVE at Fourth St. – DRydock 4-0667

ele der Mamen' ['A Letter to Mama,' an East-Side favorite], the whole audience found it impossible to hold back their tears. No matter if the scene was laid in the hot sandy desert or the Halls of the Inquisition, Thomashefsky always managed to get a song in about Mama."

Some members of the community found these theatrics embarrassing, and hoped to create a more refined stage. A more sophisticated theater did grow up alongside the melodramatic one—but both eventually faded as the number of Yiddish speakers continued to decline and New York Jews entered mainstream American theatrical life.

THE YIDDISH PRESS

The Yiddish press was the other powerful voice of the Jewish New York experience, and the city's Yiddish newspapers were the liveliest and largest in the world. By 1915, New York had five Yiddish newspapers publishing daily, with a combined circulation that approached 500,000.

The Yiddish dailies—among them the *Morgen Zhurnal, Yiddishe Tageblat, Tog*, and *Warheit*—represented a variety of political and cultural sensibilities. The most successful and influential was the *The Jewish Daily Forward*, the *Forverts*, edited by the complex, fascinating character Abraham Cahan.

Cahan, a Russian intellectual who was both a devoted socialist and a trained Hebrew teacher, came to the United States at the age of twenty-one in 1882. He taught himself English and developed such fluency that he published well-regarded short stories and novels in his adopted language.

With the *Forverts*, which he edited for nearly half a century, Cahan worked to inform, excite, incite, and educate New York's Yiddish-speaking masses. His newspaper agitated for labor unions and socialist candidates,

(Opposite left) *The Rabbi's Family* played in the 2,000-seat People's Theater. (Opposite right) *Mosbiach Kumt* [Messiah Arrives], starring Ludwig Satz, advertised itself as a "masterful, stupendous, sensational, thrilling" musical. (Right) Bertha Gersten, Yiddish actor, at a costume ball wearing a dress made from the Yiddish newspaper *Tog* (The Day). Her best-known role was Mirele Efros, *The Jewish Queen Lear*.

explained American practices such as baseball and women's rights, and published original works by Yiddish creative writers. These influential scribes included poet Morris Rosenfeld and novelists I. J. Singer and his brother Isaac Bashevis Singer.

Probably Cahan's most popular move was publishing an advice column called "A Bintel Brief"—a bundle of letters. In this column he allowed readers to give voice to their experiences, worries, and troubles. The letters are vivid and often moving. Cahan frequently wrote responses to these letters, many of which seem extraordinarily apt.

"I am a young man of twenty-five, and I recently met a fine girl. She

has a flaw, however—a dimple in her chin. It is said that people who have this lose their first husband or wife. I love her very much, but I'm afraid to marry her lest I die because of the dimple.

"ANSWER: The tragedy is not that the girl has a dimple in her chin, but that some people have a screw loose in their heads."

The *Forverts* and its competitors helped their readers navigate the Americanization process. In the end the very success of these varied periodicals sealed their collective fate. The following generation of readers, now thoroughly Americanized, had no need for—or even the ability to read—a Yiddish

(Above) A hand-printed version of the *Forverts*'s famous letters and advice column, "A Bintel Brief." Photograph by Harvey Wang, 1987.

newspaper. Ultimately, these papers were outstanding advocates for their audiences and that is their true legacy.

As of this writing, the Yiddish *Forverts* survives, though no longer a daily and with a rapidly shrinking circulation. Currently, it has two sister publications—an English-language weekly *Forward* and a Russian-language version. The Russian edition currently has a thriving circulation, thanks to the newest Jewish immigrants in New York.

NEW YORK CITY'S JEWISH ARTISTS

Jewish New Yorkers have become celebrated writers, artists, and performers. Whether it is the particular alchemy of New York's never-ending, always-moving frenetic pace, the city's ethnic richness, or the extra element of the Jewish experience in New York, the result has been a record of outstanding artistic achievement.

The Broadway Stage: New York's Jewish composers and playwrights reinvented American musical theater. Imagine Broadway without Rodgers and Hammerstein (and don't forget Hart!), Frank Loesser, Lerner and Loewe, Irving Berlin, George and Ira Gershwin, Harold Arlen, Yip Harburg, Jerome Kern, Comden and Green, and Stephen Sondheim, for starters.

Comedians/Entertainers: American humor—theater, film, television—would have lost much of its punch without Groucho, Chico, and Harpo Marx, Milton Berle, Fanny Brice, George Burns, Sid Caesar, Eddie Cantor, Judy Holliday, Zero Mostel, Henny Youngman, and even, yes, The Three Stooges (Larry Fine, Moe Horwitz, and Jerome "Curly" Horwitz). The tradition continued with New York natives Danny Kaye and Phil Silvers in the 1950s and '60s, Woody Allen and Mel Brooks in the '70s and '80s, and Jerry Seinfeld in the 1990s.

(Above) Alvie Singer (Woody Allen), noted neurotic New York Jew, and Annie Hall (Diane Keaton) chat on the street in *Annie Hall*, 1977.

American Literature: The first celebrated Jewish New York writers were *Forverts* editor Cahan and Lower East Siders Henry Roth and Michael Gold, whose novels (respectively) *The Rise of David Levinsky, Call It Sleep*, and *Jews Without Money* were masterpieces of immigrant literature. Second- and third-generation New York Jewish writers were even more plentiful and successful. A small sampling includes Isaac Asimov, Joseph Heller, Lillian Hellman, Alfred Kazin, Norman Mailer, Bernard Malamud, Arthur Miller, Grace Paley, Dorothy Parker, J. D. Salinger—and even that late-in-life New Yorker Isaac Bashevis Singer.

Painting and Sculpture: The visual arts had not been a traditional Jewish pursuit but they flowered among Jewish New Yorkers.

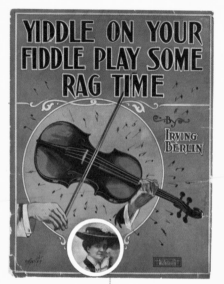

Distinguished painters with a New York pedigree included Barnett Newman, Mark Rothko, Leonard Baskin, Peter Blume, Philip Evergood, and the three Soyer brothers—Moses, Raphael, and Isaac. Other distinguished New York-raised or trained Jewish artists included painters Helen Frankenthaler, William Gropper, Lee Krasner, Roy Lichtenstein, Louis Lozowick, Larry Rivers, and Max Weber, and world-renowned sculptors Louise Nevelson, Jo Davidson, Eva Hesse, and Chaim Gross.

This is an honor roll that any nation would be proud to have produced. Incredibly, it represents only a portion of the output—of a portion of the population—of one city. This is what Jewish New Yorkers have created over the last one hundred years. And more, surely, is to come.

(Above) Irving Berlin grew up on the Lower East Side, where his father was a part-time cantor. Berlin's 1908 "Yiddle on Your Fiddle" linked Jewish music with Ragtime. (Opposite) New York's golden boy George Gershwin, painted by New Yorker William Auerbach-Levy. Born Jacob Gershovitz, Gershwin brought pop music into the classical concert hall.

"Goodbye, God, I'm going to America!" was a wisecrack heard by Eastern European immigrants leaving their intensely religious communities for the seemingly secular world of New York City. There was certainly an element of truth to the glib phrase as the immigrants were journeying to a city with no tradition of Jewish scholarship or piety. For nearly 200 years, not one ordained rabbi presided in New York City, and until the 1840s, laymen led Jewish services. Without a chief rabbi, there was no one to pass judgment on religious infractions. And from the 1880s on, the city was filled with antireligious sentiment from Jewish socialists, freethinkers, and communists.

But despite its reputation for exalting progress over piety, New York City offered those Jews who desired to do so a place to pray, practice, and even reinvent their religion without fear of brutal attack. In this congenial environment, Judaism flourished. The city eventually gave rise to hundreds of synagogues, three rabbinical seminaries, numerous yeshivas, a Yeshiva University, and dozens of other religious institutions.

Today, New York City offers something for every type and facet of Jewish religious life. Unique places of worship in the city cater to Jews of diverse national origins, linguistic traditions, styles of worship, philosophical affiliations, and even

(Above) Interior, Eldridge Street Synagogue. This great shul is now being renovated after years of neglect. Photograph by Richard Berenholtz.
(Opposite) Sofer (Torah Scribe) at work, Essex Street, Lower East Side, during the 1980s. Photograph by Harvey Wang.

professions. A sampling of synagogues in Manhattan includes: a Millinery Center Synagogue, Garment Center Congregation, Actors Temple, Fur Center Synagogue, Gay and Lesbian Synagogue, Romaniote (Greek-speakers) synagogue, Romanian-American congregation, Austrian Shul, Sephardic (Levantine/Middle Eastern) synagogue, Sephardic (Spanish and Portuguese) synagogue, and Reconstructionist synagogues. One can also find an African Hebrew congregation, a Congregation for Humanistic Judaism, a Temple of Universal Judaism, the Reconstructionist Society for the Advancement of Judaism, a Jewish Continuity Center, and congregations of Jews from Bialystok, Lisk, and many other towns and shtetlach.

THE ONLY SYNAGOGUE IN TOWN

Imagine, then, that until 1825, the only synagogue in all of New York City was Shearith Israel, the "Spanish and Portuguese congregation" that began in 1654 with those twenty-three refugees from South America. Though Director-General Stuyvesant begrudgingly allowed them to stay, he forbade the Jews to pray in public, insisting that they congregate in private homes for religious worship and ceremonies. However, the English conquered New Amsterdam soon afterwards, and New York map of 1695 already included a notation for a "Jews Synagogue."

In the late 1720s, the small Jewish community of New York (about thirty Jewish households) built its first synagogue on Mill Street in lower Manhattan. As the community was not particularly affluent, members appealed to richer Jewish communities in the Caribbean, requesting financial assistance for construction.

By 1730, congregation members of Shearith Israel conducted services on Mill Street in the Spanish-and-Portuguese ritual and language. Some ninety years later, Ashkenazic Jews from England, the German states, and Poland outnumbered the congregation's old-line Dutch/Spanish and Portuguese Sephardic Jews. In 1825, a group of these Ashkenazim, unhappy with Sephardic ritual, took a fateful step and proclaimed their independence. They soon established New York City's second synagogue, Congregation B'nai Jeshurun.

It was not long before other groups decided they needed their own houses of worship. Three years later, a group of mostly German Jews broke off from B'nai Jeshurun to form Anshe Chesed. Many more congregations were soon to follow—including Rodeph Sholom, Ohev Sholom, Shaarey Tefilah, and Shaarey Hashamayim—all heralding the establishment of a new Jewish religious order in New York City.

The fragmentation of religious institutions did not spell the end of Shearith Israel, however. Even with the secession of many congregants, the oldest synagogue in New York City still retained members from a variety of backgrounds.

When German-born Isaac Mayer Wise explored New York synagogues in 1846, he bemusedly noted, "The Portuguese congregation was the oldest, and the oldest Portuguese was a Polish Jew."

By 1860, New York had more than two dozen synagogues, including Bohemian, Dutch, English, French, and Russian-Polish congregations. However, the explosive growth wasn't solely a result of the city's increasing number of Jews or their differing national origins. The expansion also reflected a major philosophical schism in Jewish society. German "Hebrews" were now the largest group of Jews in New York City, and they had developed a less tradition-bound form of their faith, Reform Judaism.

These reformers sought to update the practice of Judaism for the scientific age. Reform introduced family seating (men and women together), services in modern languages, and in general rejected the "unchanging nature" of Jewish law. Followers introduced a choir and an organ into the service, and for a time held Sabbath services on Sundays rather than Saturdays. One outcome of Reform Judaism was to create a religious practice that

(Above) Black Jews of Harlem: perhaps as many as 3,000 African-American Jews worship at synagogues in Harlem, Brooklyn, and the Bronx.

seemed less exotic and alien to Christian Americans.

New York's first Reform temple, Emanu-El, was founded in 1845. At the congregation's initial meeting, the impoverished German immigrants raised a grand total of $28.25 among them. However, by 1868, Emanu-El had become "the congregation of the German Jewish investment bankers and merchant princes," wrote historian Charles Silberman. Just twenty-three years after that meager fundraising meeting, the sale of pews for a new building raised more than $700,000!

Most Jewish New Yorkers in the 1870s were of German origin, and most belonged to one of the numerous Reform congregations. The late nineteenth century brought New York an influx of Orthodox Jews from Eastern Europe. When these "shtetl" Jews arrived, they were stunned by the different forms of Judaism they found. Most of the

(Above left) Jewish women praying tashlich service on the Williamsburg Bridge, Rosh Hashanah, 1909. (Above right) Purim "Fancy Dress" Masquerade Balls were a highlight of the Jewish social scene. The proceeds of this March 1881 event supported the Hebrew Orphan Asylum building fund.

newest immigrants perceived these new forms of their religion "little better than heathenism," in the words of sociologist/historian Nathan Glazer. Inevitably, this led to great conflict and misunderstanding between German and Russian Jews for decades to come.

The schism between Orthodox and Reform Jews ultimately led to a third way: the Conservative movement. The movement aimed to keep traditional Jewish practice yet also adapt to contemporary American life. It began in New York City in 1885 with the founding of the Jewish Theological Seminary (JTS), but the seminary did not thrive until 1902, when Rabbi Solomon Schecter came from Cambridge University to New York to assume the JTS presidency. Schecter was a highly respected Jewish scholar and his vigorous leadership laid the groundwork for the world-class institution that JTS has now become in its West 122nd Street headquarters.

(Above) A 1915 postcard of a Lower East Side family praying tashlich, with the Brooklyn Bridge in the background. (Right) Rosh Hashanah greeting card, c. 1910.

CHANGES IN RELIGIOUS OBSERVANCE

Even as the religious divide widened between Reform and Orthodox Jews, the level of observance of the newly arrived Eastern Europeans began to drop dramatically. While numerous "Russian" Jews struggled to remain faithful to religious rules, many others gave up at least some of their practices. One factor was economic necessity: many Jewish employees felt they had to work on the Sabbath in order to keep their jobs and earn enough to support their families. But even Jewish shopkeepers, who had more control over their hours, ignored the injunction to abstain from work on Shabbat. A 1913 police survey found that nearly 60 percent of stores in two heavily Jewish precincts of the Lower East Side were remaining open on Judaism's traditional day of rest. The other factor in the relaxation of religious observance was big-city anonymity. The powerful force

of community disapproval—nearly all-encompassing in small town Europe—was mostly ineffective in the brimming metropolis.

Clearly, in this new Jewish society, many Jews could not—or would not—be bound by tradition's timetable. However, unlike many labor and socialist leaders, the majority of Jewish workers did not give up their practices happily or easily. Many workers continued, even to their disadvantage, to honor some of the customs most important to them. "It was they, in their great numbers, who crowded the Orthodox synagogs [sic] that were opened after 1882 by the scores and hundreds," wrote historian Bezalel Sherman.

New immigrants from Turkey, Greece, and the Balkans—the poor "Levantine" Jews—also ended up working on Shabbat, notes Sephardi rabbi and historian Marc Angel. Despite the break from old-country traditions, the Levantine Jews also looked to create

---

(Above left) Levantine Jews put on an elaborate Purim play, Lower East Side, 1936.

synagogues of their own. In 1913, high holiday services were held for immigrants by societies from Constantinople (98 Forsyth St), Gallipoli (83 Forsyth St), the Greek communities of Rhodes (281 Grand St), Kastoria (79-81 Forsyth St.), and Monastir, Yugoslavia (98 Forsyth St), among others.

YOM KIPPUR BALLS

New York's synagogues, both grand and modest, overflowed with observant Jews on the holiest day of the Jewish year, Yom Kippur. Even the most irreligious succumbed to the powerful Day of Atonement.

There were some, however, who did resist the Yom Kippur's aura of

holiness, going so far as to even mock the very idea. Many political radicals and freethinkers around the turn of the twentieth century commemorated Yom Kippur by throwing grand celebrations known as Yom Kippur Balls.

Nonobservers rented halls, engaged musicians, and distributed fliers to Lower East Side workers and patrons. A ticket to one such blasphemous event, translated in the *New York Sun* on September 24, 1890, read: "Grand Yom Kippur Ball with theatre. Arranged with the consent of all new rabbis of liberty. Kol Nidre Night and Day in the year 6851 (5651), after the invention of the Jewish idols, and 1890, after the birth of the false

(Above) Mashgiach Naftalie Lichtenstein at the Pupa & Zehlem Matzo Bakery, Williamsburg, New York. Photograph by Harvey Wang, 1987.
(Following spread) The spectacular interior of the reform Central Synagogue, the oldest synagogue (opened 1872) in continuous use in New York City. Photograph by Richard Berenholtz.

Messiah. . . . Music, dancing, buffet, Marseillaise and other hymns against Satan."

The angry assault on religion did not go over well with many Jews, however, even those who were not observant. Looking back many years later, an anarchist leader reflected, "The war against God . . . played a great part in the decrease of anarchist influence in Jewish life."

TODAY'S TEMPLES AND SHULS

Today, New York City synagogues range from the stately to the shteibel (tiny storefront rooms where some Orthodox congregations pray). Temple Emanu-El on Fifth Avenue is the largest Reform temple in the world, seating more than 2,500 worshippers. Other grand, historic synagogues with downtown roots, such as Central Synagogue and Rodeph Sholom, continue to flourish uptown.

The Lower East Side's Jewish community is tiny now, but it is still home to places of great historic significance. The Eldridge Street Synagogue, America's first great Orthodox shul built by Eastern European Jews, is a prime example. Opened in 1887, its first rabbi was Isaac Gellis, whose relatives went on to build a food business in his name. Among the many notables who prayed at the Eldridge Street Synagogue were entertainers and actors Al Jolson, Eddie Cantor, Edward G. Robinson, and Sam Jaffe, medical scientists Jonas Salk and Linus Pauling, and artist Ben Shahn.

On the high holidays till about 1915, the Eldridge Street congregation drew thousands of worshippers, and police were called in to help manage the crowds on the narrow streets. Sadly, in the 1930s, as the Jewish population of the Lower East Side plummeted, the congregation dispersed and the building fell into disrepair. It was not until the 1980s that historical preservationists established a foundation to rescue the structure. Today, there are efforts to restore the shul, and its impressive façade still dominates the cramped side street where it

(Above) The oldest Jewish congregation in North America—Shearith Israel—now prays in its grand 1897 building on Central Park West. Photograph by Richard Berenholtz.

is located. The aging symbol of downtown Jewish life is mere blocks away from Shteibel Row, where more than fifteen mini-synagogues line East Broadway.

The Park Avenue Synagogue, affiliated with the Conservative movement, seats more than 1,000 in its building on 87th Street. B'nai Jeshurun, New York City's second-oldest Jewish congregation, is now located on the Upper West Side, about a mile away from the city's oldest, Shearith Israel. B'nai Jeshurun's congregation has grown so large that it now prays not only in its beautiful 1918 synagogue but also shares space in nearby St. Paul and St. Andrew's Lutheran Church.

The Upper West Side is also home to a thriving young orthodox community, and on the Simchat Torah holiday, the neighborhood streets fill with hundreds of joyous dancers. Jewish prayer, once perhaps seen as endangered, is very much alive and well in early twenty-first century New York.

(Above) The Park East Synagogue on East 67 Street, built in 1888 by Orthodox congregants from Germany. Photograph by Richard Berenholtz.

Chapter Eight
LEADER OF WORLD JEWRY

"Every call for aid from stricken Jews in other parts of the world revivified Jewish life in New York by reminding New York Jews of their own people."

—HYMAN GRINSTEIN

In 1840, New York City's small Jewish community was outraged by news from Damascus: Officials were arresting Syrian Jews and torturing them in order to elicit a confession to a supposed ritual murder. New York's Jews staged a protest rally and called upon the American government to intercede with the Ottoman Sultan. In response, President Martin van Buren instructed the American consul in Damascus to seek protection for the Jews of that city. This was perhaps the first time that New York Jews, then numbering just 15,000, mobilized to protect a Jewish community abroad. It was an auspicious, if modest, beginning of what would become a significant, and ongoing, concern.

Throughout the violent twentieth century, Jewish New Yorkers have provided an astonishing level of aid to protect and defend World Jewry. The traumatic events abroad had great personal resonance, as New York Jews heard reports of family and friends they left behind now suffering in the "old countries." But even those with no family ties recognized the community's responsibility to provide relief for endangered Jews the world over.

Over the years, New York City's Jewish organizations have collected staggering amounts of money for aid. Their donations

(Above) This furrier—and many other members of the Jewish-dominated New York City fur industry—donated his services one day a week to make fur-lined vests for U.S. servicemen during World War II. (Opposite) Six young women with pushkes and sashes asking for donations for the Central Committee to help poor European Jews, 1919.

supplied food, medicine, and miscellaneous items to those seeking evacuation and resettlement in the United States and Israel. The seemingly endless list of Jewish catastrophes during the twentieth century includes upheaval and starvation across Eastern Europe after World War I, the murder of six million Jews in the Holocaust of World War II, the captive Jewish communities of the Soviet Union, and for the past fifty-plus years, various threats to the state of Israel. Commencing with World War I, Jewish New Yorkers began rallying for support for their fellow Jews around the world and have not stopped since.

LIONS AND LAMBS UNITE TO AID THE SHTETL

World War I was a disaster for shtetl Jews from its inception. As early as the summer of 1914, tens of thousands of Jewish civilians on the German-Polish-Russian eastern front were trapped amidst fierce fighting. Hostile armies forced Jews to evacuate their villages, and to undertake a harrowing search for food and shelter across a war zone.

New York City's Orthodox community reacted quickly, collecting money and creating a relief committee within days of getting the news. As a contemporary observer pointed out, "The victims . . . are their own blood relatives. The funds which they collected went directly to care for the comfort of the brothers and sisters and the fathers and mothers of the donors."

Two other major relief efforts soon got underway. In one, businessman and community leader Louis Marshall brought affluent Jews of the philanthropic community together. In the other, working-class labor unions created emergency fund drives and organized relief efforts. Within a year, these three sectors (the Orthodox, wealthy philanthropists, and the unions) set aside their vast philosophical differences and merged into what eventually became known as the American Jewish Joint Distribution Committee (JDC). In the

(Above) From the 1920s through the 1950s, Jewish homes seemed incomplete without a blue pushke box for donations to Keren Kayemet (the Jewish National Fund).
(Opposite left) An evocative poster from the New York-based Jewish Relief Campaign, which sent millions of dollars in aid to Eastern European Jews caught in World War I. 1917.

ensuing years, the JDC would become a principal source of assistance and aid to Jews worldwide. "The Jewish lions lay down with the lambs to help out other Jews whose plight was desperate," wrote historian Jacob Rader Marcus. In 1917 alone, the Orthodox raised $2 million, the unions $1 million, and the philanthropists $9 million, for a total of $12 million!

As World War I raged, the Russian Revolution took place, resulting in the collapse of political authority in Eastern Europe. The subsequent chaos led to starvation, disease, pogroms, and hundreds of thousands of fatalities across the land. Massive violence against Jews in Eastern Europe included more than 1,500 documented incidents between 1919 and 1921. Thankfully, the JDC was well established

(Above) United Jewish Appeal poster, c. 1947, promotes tzedakah—
"righteous action," or charity—for Jewish communities around the world.

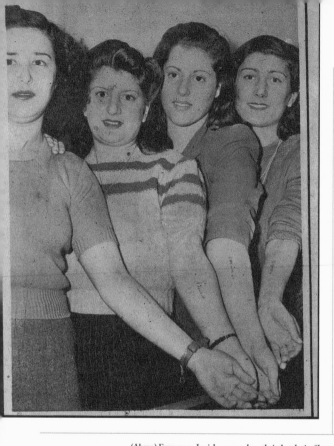

by this point and quickly sent millions of dollars of food and supplies overseas.

The Levantine Jewish population created their own Sephardic Relief committees on the Lower East Side. The groups responded to disasters in their part of the world; for example, when the fire of 1918 in Salonika devastated the area and when the Turkish-Greek war of 1922–23 threatened the Jews of Smyrna.

The passage of restrictive immigration laws in the 1920s and the growth of European anti-Semitism in subsequent years created great concern amongst the Jews of New York. Through a variety of efforts, relief organizations were able to bring a tiny segment of the endangered population—perhaps 50,000 Jews—to New York from Europe during the 1930s.

Locally, New York's Jews had always been aware of genteel anti-Semitism by such institutions as banks, corporations, and law firms that were notoriously unwilling to hire Jews. Discrimination also existed in "sensibly restricted" housing developments around the city. It was during the 1930s, however, that numerous isolated

(Above) Four young Jewish women show their Auschwitz "horror-camp" tattooed numbers to a *Forverts* photographer, c. 1945.
A stunned New York community took in thousands of survivors in the post-war years.

incidents—swastikas and graffiti scrawled on homes and businesses, an occasional smashed storefront or physical attack—reminded the Jewish community of the far graver dangers faced by Jews in Europe. When the Nazis pressed their "final solution" against the Jews during World War II, New York Jewish families were excruciatingly aware of the vulnerability of those they had left behind.

The devastation that World War II wrought on European Jewry—the murder of one-third of the world's Jews—was further attested to by the number of concentration camp survivors who arrived in New York during the late 1940s and early 1950s. Stark photographs of survivors, such as young women displaying tattooed numbers on their arms and newly arrived siblings who had lost their parents, appeared regularly in the Yiddish press during those post-war years.

new York World's fair 1939

135:—JEWISH PALESTINE EXHIBIT.

The too-real reminders of what had happened to European Jews during World War II strengthened resolve among the New York Jewish community to support the recently created state of Israel. Much of that task fell to the United Jewish Appeal (UJA), an organization that had been created in 1939 in response to increasing Nazi violence against Jews. The UJA's mission was to collect funds to help Jews around the world and in the Yishuv, the Jewish community in prestatehood Palestine. In fact, the Jewish community in Palestine, despite the storm clouds of the coming war, produced a pavilion at the 1939–40 New York City World's Fair.

During the post-war years of the late 1940s, UJA collected more than $100 million to aid in the resettlement of Jews and the creation of the Jewish state. Much of the focus of New York Jewish philan-

(Above) The Jews of Palestine presented exhibits about their homeland in this pavilion at New York's 1939 World's Fair.

thropy in the 1950s was on the building of the state of Israel, which was absorbing Jews from all over the world, and which engaged in another war with its Arab neighbors in 1956. It was the 1967 Arab–Israeli war, which was preceded by weeks of international tension, which really demonstrated the depth of New York Jewry's support for the state of Israel. In a matter of a few weeks, the city's Jewish community raised $72 million. Six years later, in response to the 1973 Israel–Arab war, the donations topped $100 million.

Ongoing efforts to streamline the collection and dissemination of funds to needy Jews in New York and the world over resulted in the merger in 1986 of the Federation of Jewish Philanthropies and the United Jewish Appeal. Today, UJA-Federation is the face of "Official Jewish New York"—an extraordinary coalition of Jewish charities and service organizations.

For the past one hundred years, Jewish New York has grown into a world center of Jewish life, Jewish thought, and Jewish power. New York Jewry has fulfilled completely the mandate the Dutch West Indies Company set out for Jews here 350 years ago: "not to become a burden . . . but be supported by their own nation." New York now is a leading voice of the Jewish international community.

In today's world, in which an independent but still threatened Jewish state exists, New York Jews know full well that their attention to the needs of World Jewry is incredibly important. Beyond that is the community's keen awareness that Jews the world over are linked, and that living in the freest, most affluent Jewish society in the world does release them from responsibility for their brothers and sisters.

(Left) The Museum of Jewish Heritage overlooks the harbor of lower Manhattan, not far from where the first Jews arrived in 1654. Photograph by Richard Berenholtz.
(Right) The former Warburg mansion on Fifth Avenue is now home to one of the world's greatest collections of Judaica, the Jewish Museum. Photograph by Richard Berenholtz.

GLOSSARY

The lively language of Jewish New York could easily fill its own book, but here are definitions of some common words used in this book. Transliterations are from Yiddish or other non-English languages, so spellings may differ slightly from source to source.

Ashkenazi (pl. Ashkenazim) — Hebrew for "One from Germany." Refers to Jews who come from (or whose ancestors came from) Germany, Eastern Europe, or, often, Western Europe.

Challah — Special bread, made with eggs, usually braided, and served on Shabbat and holidays.

Kashruth — The system of regulations regarding which foods are kosher (permitted to observant Jews).

Kibbe — Fried food from Middle Eastern countries, brought to New York by Levantine Jews. Made of bulghur, mixed with meat, lamb, or vegetables.

Kibitz — Banter or joking talk. (Not to be confused with "kibbutz," an Israeli cooperative farm.)

Kibitzers — Those who engage in kibitzing.

Kippah — Hebrew for skullcap.

Knish — A small, baked "cake," no bigger than the palm of one's hand, usually stuffed with potato (or cheese, vegetable, or fruit).

Kol Nidre — Hebrew, literally "All Vows." Term for the service, and a major prayer of that service, on the eve of Yom Kippur (Day of Atonement).

Kosher — Foods that may be eaten. Also used to mean "proper."

Ladino — Language based on medieval Spanish, written in Hebrew letters, and spoken by some Sephardi Jews.

Levantine — Jews from Mediterranean countries.

Mashgiach — One who certifies that food is kosher—prepared in accordance with kashruth.

Purim — Festive holiday when Jews celebrate their rescue from threatened slaughter by Haman, a Persian official.

Pushke — Small box used to collect coins for charity.

Rosh Hashanah — Jewish New Year, celebrated in September or October.

Sephardi (pl. Sephardim) — Hebrew for "one from Spain." Refers to Jews whose ancestors were banished from Spain and Portugal during early years of the Inquisition (1492–1500s). Most moved to Holland or Mediterranean countries (Turkey, Greece, Morocco, etc.).

Shabbat — Hebrew for Sabbath, Friday night to Saturday night, when abstaining from labor is prescribed by Jewish law.

Shabbes — Yiddish for Shabbat (Sabbath).

Shmata — Yiddish for "rags," loosely interpreted to mean "clothing," and, often, the garment trade.

Shteibel — Small space, often a storefront room, in which prayers are conducted by Orthodox Jews.

Shtetl (pl. shtetlach) — Yiddish for "small town," referring to the Jewish villages that dotted Eastern Europe.

Shul — Yiddish for "school," used generally to mean "synagogue," especially Orthodox synagogues.

Tashlich — Hebrew term, literally "casting off," which refers to the ritual observed on the first day of Rosh Hashanah. The ritual involves going to a moving body of water and throwing pieces of bread or other items into it. Symbolic of casting away one's sins.

Tsouris — Yiddish for "trouble."

Tzedakah — Hebrew word best translated as "Righteousness," and referring to the obligation to help others ("charity" and "justice" are other translations).

Yarmulkah — The term used in Yiddish for skullcap.

Yiddish — Medieval, German-based language written with Hebrew letters and spoken by most Jews across Eastern Europe.

Yom Kippur — Holiest day of the Jewish religious year, when Jews confess and atone for their sins.

LIST OF ILLUSTRATIONS

✧ ✧ ✧ ✧ ✧ ✧ ✧

Page 51. Harvey Wang. Photograph of Mark Russ Federman of Russ and Daughters store. 1993

Page 51. Richard Berenholtz. Photograph of exterior of Zabar's

Page 52. Vintage label of Kedem Wine. Collection of Peter Schweitzer

Page 52. Vintage label of Schapiro's Honey Wine. Collection of Peter Schweitzer

Page 53. Marjory Collins. Rabbi in kosher wine shop in the Jewish section of New York City. c. 1942. Photograph. Library of Congress, Prints and Reproductions Division

Page 54. Men in classroom at the Educational Alliance. Photograph. From the Archives of the YIVO Institute for Jewish Research

Page 55. Yeshiva University, Wils campus in Washington Heights. Courtesy of Dept. of Communications and Public Affairs.

Page 56. Photo by Budd. Moses Soyer painting portrait of Chaim Gross. Photograph. The Educational Alliance, New York City

Page 58. Americanization Day at the Educational Alliance. Before 1914. Photograph. From the Archives of the YIVO Institute for Jewish Research

Page 59. Classroom with children. Before 1914. Photograph. From the Archives of the YIVO Institute for Jewish Research

Page 60. Vintage postcard of The Hebrew Orphan Asylum. Courtesy Seymour B. Durst Old York Library at The Graduate Center of The City University of New York

Page 61. Educational Alliance Legal Aid Bureau. 1920s or 30s. Photograph. From the Archives of the YIVO Institute for Jewish Research

Page 64. Vintage postcard of Boris Thomashefsky's Roumanian Village. Collection of Peter Schweitzer

Page 65. Jacob Epstein. Spirit of the Ghetto. 1902. Courtesy Seymour B. Durst Old York Library at The Graduate Center of The City University of New York

Page 66. Portrait of Molly Picon. 1949. Photograph. Forms part of: New York World-Telegram and the Sun Newspaper Photograph Collection. Library of Congress, Prints and Reproductions Division

Page 67. Vintage postcard of The Ensemble of Thomashefsky's Roumanian Village, 181 Allen Street, New York City (front and back). Collection of Peter Schweitzer

Page 68. Theater poster for The Rabbi's Family. American Jewish Historical Society, Waltham, Mass., and New York City

Page 68. Theater poster for Moshiach Kumt. American Jewish Historical Society, Waltham, Mass., and New York City

Page 69. Bertha Gersten, in Prize-winning costume at yearly costume ball, a Yiddish newspaper tradition. Photograph. Museum of the City of New York

Page 70. Harvey Wang. Photograph of the Bintel Brief from Forverts. 1987

Page 71. Woody Allen and Diane Keaton in Annie Hall. 1977. Photograph. © Bettmann/CORBIS

Page 72. Sheet music of Irving Berlin's Yiddle on Your Fiddle Play Some Rag Time. 1908. American Jewish Historical Society, Waltham, Mass., and New York City

Page 73. William Auerbach Levy. George Gershwin at the Piano. 1926. Oil on canvas. Museum of the City of New York. Gift of Max Levy

Page 74. Harvey Wang. Photograph of Torah scribe on Essex Street

Page 75. Richard Berenholtz. Photograph of Eldridge Street Synagogue

Page 77. Black Jews of Harlem. Photograph. From the Archives of the YIVO Institute for Jewish Research

Page 78. Jews praying on Williamsburg Bridge, New York City, on New Year's Day. 1909. Photograph. George Grantham Bain Collection. Library of Congress, Prints and Reproductions Division

Page 78. Invitation to Purim "Fancy Dress Ball." 1881. American Jewish Historical Society, Waltham, Mass., and New York City

Page 79. From The Golden Age of Jewish Postcards: 1895-1920. Jewish New Year card. c. 1915. American Jewish Historical Society, Waltham, Mass., and New York City

Page 79. Photograph of Ida Mass. Personalized Jewish New Year card. Early twentieth century. Collection of Alvin Mass

Page 80. Cast of a Purim Play. 1936. Photograph. Collection of Yeshiva University Museum. Gift of Mrs. Adatto Schlesinger

Page 81. Harvey Wang. Photograph of Mashgiach Naftalie Lichtenstein. 1987

Pages 82 & 83. Richard Berenholtz. Photograph of Central Synagogue

Page 84. Richard Berenholtz. Photograph of Shearith Israel

Page 85. Richard Berenholtz. Photograph of Park East Synagogue

Page 86. Central Relief Committee. Six Women with Pushkes and sashes. 1919. Photograph. Archives of the YIVO Institute for Jewish Research

Page 87. Marjory Collins. Jewish fur worker. December, 1942. Photograph. Library of Congress, Prints and Reproductions Division

Page 88. Blue pushke donation box. Early twentieth century. Jewish National Fund

Page 89. Johnstone Bruke Studios. Share-Jewish Relief Campaign poster. 1917. Original lithograph by Sackett & Wilhelms Corporation, Brooklyn. Library of Congress, Prints and Reproductions Division

Page 89. Fodor. "Their Fight Is Our Fight—United Jewish Appeal" poster. c. 1940s. Collection of Yeshiva University Museum

Page 90. Women displaying tattoos in the Forvets. c. 1945. Photograph. Archives of the YIVO Institute for Jewish Research

Page 91. Vintage postcard of Jewish Palestine Exhibit at the New York World's Fair. 1939. Collection of Yeshiva University Museum, New York

Page 92. Richard Berenholtz. Photograph of the The Museum of Jewish Heritage

Page 92. Richard Berenholtz. Photograph of The Jewish Museum New York

Page 96. Sister and brother refugees of World War II. 1951. Photograph. Archives of the YIVO Institute for Jewish Research

Front cover: Vintage postcard of Essex and Hester Streets, early 1900s. Brown Brothers photo. The New York Public Library Picture Collection

Half title page. 175 Ludlow Street. 1934. Photograph. American Jewish Historical Society, Waltham, Mass., and New York City

Title page. Young women drawing at the Educational Alliance Art School. c. 1920s. Photograph. The Educational Alliance

Survivors in New York: French-Jewish siblings, their parents killed in the Holocaust, were brought here by the JDC in 1951.